Demon Slayers

Demon Slayers

Paul Hollis, Ph.D.
Claire Hollis, Ph.D.

DEMON SLAYERS

ISBN 0-9673122-1-3
Library of Congress Catalog Card Number: 99-96602
Copyright (c) 1999 by Warfare Publications
Printed in the United States of America

Published by: Warfare Publications
                  PMB #206
                  4577 Gunn Highway
                  Tampa, FL 33624 USA
                  (813) 265-2379
                  Fax: (813) 908-0228
                  E-mail: WarfareP@aol.com
                  Web site: www.warfareplus.com

Cover Design: Norm Brubaker

Unless otherwise indicated, all scripture references are from
the authorized *King James Version* of the Bible.

The Lord has ALL AUTHORITY AND POWER—all He needs is a mouthpiece. That is where we come in! God has chosen to use man, and you will never find in the Bible that He has a Plan B. We stress that we are merely God's mouthpieces, empowered to give commands to demons. We initiate the action of God's power and authority on this earth by speaking with our mouth the words in Jesus' Name!

NOTE:
Although satan is very prominent in this book, we do not wish to honor him in any way. For this reason, his name will be treated as a common noun and will not be capitalized in this manuscript. We consider him "lower case" and, even at the risk of being criticized for being grammatically incorrect, we will follow this procedure.

Several of the testimonies contained herein were also related in our first book, *THIS MEANS WAR.*

TABLE OF CONTENTS

DEDICATION

A lady we attended church with approached me holding a gift box. She had been through our deliverance program and knew that I was writing a book.

The box contained a large bottle shaped like a heart, filled with olive oil. It was sealed with a cork and had foil around the top of it. She said she had seen the bottle in a department store and the Lord prompted her to buy it for me. She said the Lord also told her to tell me that I should put the bottle out where I would see it constantly as a reminder to work on my book.

The morning after she bought the bottle, she noticed there was a little oil leaking from the foil seal and she wanted to take it back to the store to exchange it. However, the Lord told her that the leaking oil had significance. It was representative of the Holy Spirit and it would leak over onto everyone who reads this book. She also bought a tiny little ballpoint pen and put it around the neck of the bottle to remind me to write!

We dedicate this book to the Holy Spirit, and pray that the oil of the Holy Spirit will truly spill over on you as you read it.

Thou preparest a table before me in the presence of mine enemies: thou anointest my head with oil; my cup runneth over. Surely goodness and mercy shall follow me all the days of my life: and I will dwell in the house of the Lord forever. (Psalm 23:5,6)

FOREWORD

DR. MYLES E. MUNROE
Bahamas Faith Ministries, International

The material addressed in this work is critical to this generation, as so many disillusioned minds seek for supernatural solutions to their problems. There is a great need for this book, as it exposes the work of darkness and magnifies the power of the light of God's Spirit. *DEMON SLAYERS* is an excellent tool to help the believer deal effectively with the supernatural realm.

INTRODUCTION

DEMON SLAYERS is about making war! For too long satan and his kingdom have been beating up on the Body of Christ and there are too many wounded Christians because of lack of knowledge. This book *exposes* satan's kingdom and his tactics, and shows you how to *expel* him from your life. This book contains true accounts of encounters Christians have had while going through deliverance. We relate what happened *during* their deliverance and the victory in praise afterwards!

If you have been experiencing times in your daily spiritual walk when you seemed to become totally defeated by the devil, you need to read this book. You can find the keys to VICTORY over your enemy. This book will bring fresh enlightenment and a treasure of wisdom on HOW TO PUT THE ENEMY UNDER YOUR FEET.

THIS BOOK BRINGS
THE WAR TO THE ENEMY!

This charge I commit unto thee, son Timothy, according to the prophecies which went before on thee, that thou by them mightest war a good warfare. (I Timothy 1:18)

For the weapons of our warfare are not carnal, but mighty through God to the pulling down of strongholds. (II Cor. 10:4)

PREFACE

Paul and I do not claim to be experts and we certainly do not think we know all there is to know about the devil's kingdom! We are just vessels that God has chosen for this ministry. He probably chose us in the first place because we hadn't read all the books and fancied ourselves to be prepared for deliverance ministry. No, we knew that God would have to show us things firsthand and put us through His school of learning.

This book is not theological in nature and is not presented as a textbook. It contains true-life experiences from our files—things that actually happened to us in our deliverance sessions while demon entities were being expelled from the lives of some wonderful Christians. These individuals had been tricked, deceived, and bound up by demons trying to keep them from all that God wanted them to be. All the accounts in this book are true! We want you to read them and be encouraged, because bondage has kept the Body of Christ from accomplishing God's plan for too long!

We do not want to give the demon spirits any glory or special attention by presenting these testimonies. The only purpose of this book is to show that God Almighty, Maker of heaven and earth, is all powerful and has all authority over satan. If you have given your heart to Jesus and truly believe that He died for your sins, you are on the winning team! You can be set free, because you have that same power and authority living inside you. You will truly know that you have satan and his kingdom under your feet.

> Dressed totally in black from head to toe, the woman's eyes darted back and forth with the most violent look we had ever seen! Her wicked grin, almost as wide as her face, seemed to say tauntingly, "Now I've got you!" Her raised arm held long, sharp scissors and she made a sort of stabbing

motion with them as she spoke. This long-time satanist had dramatically changed right before our eyes from a soft-spoken, sophisticated lady into a violent, raging, vulgar animal programmed to kill!

Being brand new in deliverance ministry, we nearly went into a state of shock. In hindsight, we believe the Lord used this incident to mature us quickly—actually, we had no choice! She was the one with the lethal weapon—the scissors—and was empowered with supernatural strength. We *had* to trust God. He was our only hope of leaving that room alive! (This complete story begins on page 63)

Over the last several years of deliverance ministry, the Lord has revealed to us the following truth:

Ye are of God, little children, and have overcome them: because greater is he that is in you, than he that is in the world. (I John 4:4)

The day we encountered the woman with the scissors, we learned that the God who lives within us has *all power* over satan and his kingdom. This is logical, isn't it, because the God Who lives in us made satan and all of his kingdom. They have to bow to His authority; they have no choice in the matter. Even though we knew this biblical principle in our minds, at that moment we were pleased to see it in action!

If Christians could only get in their minds and hearts whom they are in Christ Jesus, they would never allow the enemy to terrorize them again. If they felt a spirit of fear coming over them, they could boldly say, "Spirit of fear, be gone, in the Name of Jesus! You have no authority in my life." The enemy would have to obey because of the power and authority of God that lives within us.

Every Christian needs to be giving satan a bad day so that he trembles every time he hears your voice speak the Word of God over your life.

It is vital to have a *balanced* deliverance ministry. Not too long ago there was a lot of "flakiness" in the church and it seemed like too many people "discerned" a devil every time someone sneezed, or saw a demon behind every other bush. It is very easy to get out in left field on issues, so great care has to be taken. Paul and I do read books about demonic issues, but we read at least twice as many books about the love of God and the anointing, or the blood of Jesus! Our favorite reading is always about the blood of Jesus. We are determined not to concentrate too much on the occult and related things.

Many people have told us that they practice astral projection and cast spells or put curses on people. They seem to want to make us curious, but we don't even ask them how they do it. If you delve into those things, you leave yourself wide open to developing an interest, and that can be dangerous.

Others have told us that we need to study all the things that are in the satanic bible and learn all the occult expressions and their meanings. They seem to think (and don't hesitate to tell us) that we should know all this and learn about the New Age paraphernalia in order to be knowledgeable about satan's kingdom. *I don't think so! Absolutely not!* Who cares? All we want to do is get people set free. The Lord has shown us how to close all the open doors in a person's life (which breaks any legal right that the devil had to be there in the first place) and then command the demons to leave in Jesus' Name—and they do! This is all that's important. Then we teach them how to stay free so that satan cannot re-enter.

PART ONE

THE MASTER'S PLAN

CLAIRE'S VISION

"Mom! He's on my side again."

"I am not! You're on *my* side. MOM!"

We were a "typical" Christian family on our way to church on a Sunday morning. The boys were in the backseat of the car and, as usual, they had drawn an imaginary line down the middle of the seat and challenged each other to cross over it.

"Boys, stop that right now." It was my standard response and I hardly even noticed what I said. But as I spoke, I realized that something odd was taking place. I could still hear the boys fussing and I could see the stores and houses and cars going by, but things suddenly changed. What was happening? I realized that I was seeing a clear vision—with my eyes wide open. The vision was in color and God burned it into my memory.

> **THE VISION**: I was standing looking at an army that literally covered the entire earth. Even though I was limited in how far my eyes could see, I *understood* in my spirit that the army was enormous! The soldiers formed perfect lines, were in perfect step, and wore perfect uniforms. They were marching the goose step and when they put their feet down, the WHOLE earth PULSATED.
>
> The marching army reminded me of a movie showing Hitler's army. I could feel the earth vibrating under my feet as they put their feet down in unison. As I stood watching the army, the movement of the earth felt exactly the same as it had when I was in an earthquake in California.
>
> Suddenly I saw Christ standing in front of

15

me, about ten feet to the left. His hands were on His hips and He was observing the army. I felt such fear that I ran and hid behind Christ, then when I knew I was safe behind Him, I bent and peeked out through the hole made by His bent arm. All I remember about His appearance is that His skin was tan (like a good suntan) and He had STRONG arm muscles.

"When is He ever going to say something?" I thought. "After all, this is Christ! All He would have to do is just say the word and they would all disappear."

The army was getting closer and when they got about three feet from stepping on us, I heard Christ speak (not audibly, but in my mind), "I am not going to say anything. YOU have to do the speaking!"

In total terror and desperation, I mumbled in a scared little voice, "In the Name of Jesus." Before I could say another word, the soldier to my right just popped like a balloon and disappeared. Then I looked to my left and the same thing happened. Pop! Gone! Then suddenly, another one popped—and another—and another! POP! POP! POP! Then there was total silence. The whole army had completely disappeared. I fell to my face and Christ turned around. He held a sword about five feet long and He rested it lightly first on my right shoulder and then on my left. Then He rested it on my head and said, "I anoint you to go and heal the brokenhearted and set the captives free!" I felt the weight of the sword on my head and I also felt the weight of those words.

The vision was over as suddenly as it had begun and I sat in the car stunned. Somehow we got into church and joined in the service. During the time of praise and worship, the lady standing next to me sat down, grabbed my hand, and pulled me down with her. She lifted a small vial of oil from her purse and said to me, "The Lord told me five minutes ago to anoint your hands with oil, but I was afraid of what you might think. I just didn't have enough nerve to do it. But now I feel like I *must* obey Him." Then she anointed the palms of my hands and we stood and continued to praise and worship the Lord. As I lifted my hands toward heaven, they felt like coals of fire burning. At certain times, even to this day, I still feel that same anointing.

I learned from the vision that God needs mouthpieces! Although my voice was soft, even scared, I had the authority and power of Christ inside my being—and that is what made the enemy flee. The enemy's plan was destroyed in the Name of Jesus! Every time we pray for someone's deliverance, we KNOW that it is CHRIST IN US doing the deliverance. It may be our voices, but it is HIS authority! By the way, that same power and authority is freely given to every born-again believer.

Then he called his twelve disciples together, and gave them power and authority over all devils, and to cure diseases. (Luke 9:1)

And I will give unto thee the keys of the kingdom of heaven: and whatsoever thou shalt bind on earth shall be bound in heaven: and whatsoever thou shalt loose on earth shall be loosed in heaven. (Matt. 16:19)

SATAN'S PLOY—CLAIRE

Be sober, be vigilant; because your adversary the devil, as a roaring lion, walketh about, seeking whom he may devour. (I Pet. 5:8)

The devil can see the anointing on the lives of God's children and his plan is to stop them before they can really get started! The vision we just related came to Claire about three weeks before her husband deserted her and their two children. In her own words:

When my husband announced that he was leaving me for another woman, I went into a state of total shock and disbelief, followed by great depression! How had this happened? Why had it happened? We had just refinanced our home and when he left, he took the credit cards, had his payroll checks directed to a new address, and didn't pay child support. I was left with a large debt and a little four-year-old car.

Our sons were young, only five and nine, but along with their grief and lack of understanding was a strong sense of wanting to help. On a Saturday evening we went to the ATM (automatic teller machine) to withdraw money so we could buy food and found that we were out of money. Very early the next morning, Joshua, the five-year-old, got up, went over to the neighbor's house and mowed his lawn. When I awoke, he had left $7 on my bedside table—his way of helping the family survive. In the beginning, before I found work, my two sons and I mowed lawns together in order to get enough money to eat.

My other son, Matt, seemed to cope fine during the day but each night at bedtime, he buried his head on my shoulder, dug his fingers into my back until it hurt, and sobbed as though his heart would break. This went on for at least a year and, of course, it broke my heart. But through all this, God was teaching me a valuable lesson. He wanted to show me that He was my source—not a job, not a husband, not others around me. I learned to live by *Isaiah 54:5: For thy Maker is thine husband; the Lord of hosts is his name; and thy Redeemer the Holy One of Israel; The God of the whole earth shall he be called.*

God proved Himself faithful to me in so many ways and let me know that He always watches out for His children. One week in particular, I was blessed financially. On Thursday, I went to a meeting of the Board of Directors of a prison ministry that I served on. The President of the Board gave me his business card and told me to come for an interview at his insurance company. When I unfolded the card, I realized there was money in it. I was embarrassed until he said to me, "The Lord told me to give you all the money I have in my pocket. I don't even know how much it is, but I want to obey the Lord." (It was $108 exactly.)

The following Monday, I attended a regular Bible study leadership meeting and a girl came up to me afterwards. "This is for you. The Lord told me to give you exactly $200." I was stunned and grateful. Then, when I got home, there was a letter from my pastor and enclosed was a check for $500. In the letter he told me that someone in the church congregation said the Lord had instructed them to give the money to me, but they wanted to remain anonymous. I WILL NEVER FORGET THAT WEEK! I KNOW THAT GOD WILL TAKE CARE OF HIS CHILDREN!

Later, the Lord blessed me with a good job as an insurance agent with lots of clients and plenty of business. Because of suddenly being made head of the household and taking on many responsibilities and duties, the vision the Lord had given me seemed to fade into the background. I realized later that our daily prayer should be: **Lord, realign my focus that it will match your priorities.**

PAUL AND CLAIRE MEET—CLAIRE

Being single and the sole provider for two sons presents many challenges. Many of my single friends were wandering in and out of "love" and getting engaged, then breaking the engagements. I was staying home eating popcorn and pizza, and playing canasta with my boys. My life was wonderful, while everyone around me seemed to be on a never-ending emotional roller coaster. I would never let my feet hit the floor in the morning without praying:

> *Lord, please let NO MAN come into my life*
> *except the one YOU CHOOSE. Satan, I*
> *COMMAND that you and your kingdom*
> *can bring NO man into my life.*

My course was set: serve the Lord, make a living, raise my two boys. After about five years, however, things were going to change.

I always sat toward the front of the church and didn't pay too much attention to others. One particular Sunday morning, I got up to leave and saw a man standing in the aisle toward the back of the church. When I saw him, I felt like a *green light came on!* I felt like God was saying, "This is the man I have chosen for you!" As I passed him, we shook hands.

I greeted several others, then went next door to the pizza house. A group of single people was sitting around a table and one of the women motioned for me to join them. The only vacant seat was *right next to Paul* and I gladly sat down. The place was so noisy that I could barely hear but I knew I was enjoying our conversation! And inside I kept hearing this little voice saying, "This is the man I have prepared for you." However, I disregarded the "little voice" and figured I was just thinking "good thoughts" because I was enjoying our conversation so much.

When I got up to leave, Paul got up, also. At that time I didn't even know his name and, even though I had enjoyed our conversation, I hadn't especially noticed what he looked like. In the car on the way home from church, I found myself saying to God, "If this is really YOU, then let him call me this week." One important fact to be noted: I hadn't even given him my name or my phone number, so how could he possibly call me?

Well, he called! And let me tell you, I really got excited! I knew that ... well, I *knew* that he was going to be my husband but I couldn't even picture in my mind what he looked like. I drew a total blank. Was he tall? Short? Was his hair light? Dark? This only added to the excitement I felt at getting to church the next Sunday to see what my "husband-to-be" looked like!

I knew this relationship was something God was putting together. You ask me how I knew. I knew because I had prayed every day for five long years and GOD ANSWERS PRAYER!

The next Sunday Paul asked me to go to lunch with him and we sat talking the entire afternoon, until it was time to go back to church for the evening service. The Lord did not reveal to Paul that I was the one for him until several weeks later and I was very careful during those weeks not to do anything on my own to make things happen. *I knew that God would let him know* because He had confirmed it to me and it would just be a matter of time before He confirmed it to Paul.

Shortly after we met, I looked over at Paul while we were in church and I heard these words, *"I have anointed him!"* I knew those words were coming straight from the Throne of God and I now know it is true. I have the privilege of seeing that anointing on a daily basis.

Paul and I met in July and were married in November of the same year. We were married only a few weeks when my younger son, Josh, came to me and asked, "Mom, do you think Paul is REAL or do you think he is an angel that God sent to us?" Paul isn't an angel, but he is an absolute saint and I thank God daily that He put us together.

If you are a single person and feel all alone, take this advise: WAIT ON THE LORD! PRAY EVERY DAY! It may take five or ten years, or even more, but when God puts it together, it will be right! Don't get ahead of God. God made us all and

He knows our personalities and He knows WHO IS PERFECT FOR YOU!

Wherefore they are no more twain, but one flesh. What therefore God hath joined together, let not man put asunder. (Matt. 19:6)

THE BIRTH OF OUR MINISTRY—CLAIRE

Shortly after Paul and I were married, we felt led to drive from Tampa to Orlando to attend Orlando Christian Center, a very large church pastored by Reverend Benny Hinn. So many attend the church each Sunday that they have multiple services and you have to stand in line to get a seat. Every Sunday when Paul and I entered the sanctuary and found seats, ushers immediately approached us and took us down to sit on the front row. This had never been discussed with us and we had no idea why they were doing this. We knew it could not be because we were wealthy or famous or influential—because we were not! We just accepted this as God's grace and His way of putting His stamp of approval on our choice of place to worship at that time.

During the months we attended Orlando Christian Center, Pastor Benny called me out personally three times to pray for someone who needed deliverance. One time he actually came down and took me by the hand and led me over to a woman who needed deliverance. I had absolutely no idea what to do, and I was especially nervous because everyone in the church was looking at me. A lady standing beside me began speaking in tongues loudly and Pastor Benny said to her, "Stop that! The demons can't understand tongues—tell them to get out in your own language." I wisely took this advice, as well, and the person we were praying for went limp, and quit kicking and twisting around.

Even though Paul and I continued to attend the church, Pastor Benny didn't know us by name. However, a couple of times he referred to us as "the couple from Tampa." One time we saw him in the hallway and he said to us, "I always want you to be on the front row."

When Pastor Benny called me up the first time to pray for someone, I was perplexed and discussed it with Paul in the car on the drive home. "I think Pastor Benny missed God this morning, Paul." You see, I knew I did not know anything about deliverance; actually I felt that I was probably just about the "greenest" person in the whole church when it came to the subject!

"Pastor Benny doesn't miss God," Paul replied. And suddenly God brought to my remembrance the vision I had had several years earlier. Even though it had been years, God's timing is always perfect! The desertion by my husband had been part of satan's plan to destroy me but Almighty God turned that tragic event around for His good! Because of the heartache, trials, hurts and disappointment I went through, I am in a position to understand the brokenhearted! I've been there and I know what it is!

While attending Orlando Christian Center, we met a young couple that was just beginning a church in Tampa. They invited us to begin a deliverance ministry in their church and God confirmed it to our hearts. Since we saw the first person in that congregation several years ago, people have been coming from everywhere for deliverance. Before long, we had a long list of people wanting to see us.

God taught us and gave us wisdom as our ministry developed. Even though we did not know (in the natural) what to do, it seemed like we knew exactly what to say and do (in the spiritual). This wisdom certainly did not come from us. *It had to come from God*! I sometimes think He chose us because we knew nothing and were completely open to anything He led us to do. When you are empty, He can use you.

The Spirit of the Lord is upon me, because he hath anointed me to preach the gospel to the poor; he hath sent me to heal the brokenhearted, to preach deliverance to the captives, and recovering of sight to the blind, to set at liberty them that are bruised, to preach the acceptable year of the Lord. (Luke 4:18, 19)

PAUL'S VISION

Shortly after our deliverance ministry got underway, the Lord gave me a powerful vision. Even today, this vision is so vivid in my mind that it seems as though I received it only yesterday.

In the vision I saw Claire standing with me in a beautiful, huge, two-story building. We walked up the wide, elegant staircase and noticed that the walls, floors and even the stairway were made of the most exquisite marble. When we arrived on the upper level, we saw that the ceiling was about eighty feet tall and, again, made completely of marble.

The upper level was filled with hundreds of Christians conversing in soft tones, apparently enjoying each other's company very much. When someone would sit, a soft cushioned chair would immediately appear and perfectly conform to the contour of that person's body. I recognized many people in that room.

Upon closer observation, we saw that the clothes these people had been wearing were lying on the floor and now they were clothed in white robes! Somehow we knew the trumpet of the Lord was about to sound and we were going to be home with Him!

Claire was standing about ten feet from me and I realized she was also wearing a white robe; her robe had a blue sash and there was a remarkable difference in her appearance! She appeared to be very young, about thirty years old! Then I looked down at myself and saw that I was also wearing a white robe.

Suddenly everyone began to slowly float toward the high, high ceiling of this enormous room. As we went upward, I thought, "How in the world are we going to go through that marble ceiling?" But when we came to the ceiling, we went right through it, as though it did not even exist!

WHOOSH! All at once we all took off like rockets toward heaven. When we got miles above the earth, a force slowed me down and took me back toward the earth. As I looked around, I saw Jesus behind me. He put His hands over my eyes as we approached earth, but I peeked through His fingers and saw the form of the earth, surrounded by dazzling clouds. I saw water, land, trees, and buildings and, as we gained speed, I wondered, "Where is the Lord taking me?" We arrived at earth but we did not stop; instead, we went right through earth until we came to the center and into HELL itself!

As soon as we arrived in hell, I saw something I hope I never will see again. People were in total agony and their screams were ghastly. They were clawing at the air and gnashing their teeth as they fought the torture consuming them. What a horrifying sight!

"Lord, we have to get these people out of here!" I cried out to Him. Then He turned to me, "Paul, I have called you into a ministry to set people free so they won't have to spend eternity in this place of torment."

I woke up! The vision left me so shaken that I felt like I was in a state of shock. Even though it was only three o'clock in the morning, I did no more sleeping that night. In fact, I couldn't even speak of what I had seen until ten o'clock that morning, when I shared the vision with Claire.

ONLY MOUTHPIECES—PAUL AND CLAIRE

To be perfectly honest with you, this book has very little to do with the two of us. We are really nothing but instruments of ministry. The principle element for success in deliverance work is the PERSON being prayed for and their willingness to let the demons go. The second vital element is the power of God Almighty, Ruler of the Universe, King of Kings, and

Lord of Lords, through the blood of Jesus and the power of His Name! You see, God is the One that kicks demons out! We are merely His mouthpieces, instruments that He uses. If you ever begin to think you are more than you really are, you can just hang it up! You will be dead meat and the devil will have you for lunch!

We wake up every morning and thank God that we are alive! We begin the day by praying,

Forgive us for anything we have done that displeases you in any way, Jesus. Cleanse us with the blood of Jesus by washing our mind, brain, memory, conscious, subconscious and unconscious, our body, soul, emotions, and will. Fill us with your Holy Spirit and put a guard on our mouth so that we say no more and no less than what You would have us say. We acknowledge that we have on the WHOLE ARMOR OF GOD and we are dressed for battle:

> *With the helmet of salvation*
> *With the breastplate of righteousness*
> *Our loins gird with truth*
> *Our feet shod with the gospel of peace*
> *We take the sword of the Spirit (the Word of God)*
> *The shield of faith*

We ask you, God, for supernatural

> *Faith*
> *Wisdom*
> *Knowledge*
> *Power*
> *Discernment*
> *Health*
> *Anointing*

In the Name of Jesus. Amen

We are now ready to pray for others and see what exciting things God has in store for us for the day.

PART TWO

TRUE-LIFE ENCOUNTERS

Demon Slayers

The following testimonies are true! These people have gone through our deliverance program, and the names, descriptions and sometimes even the genders have been changed to protect their privacy.

SPIRIT GUIDES

Everyone comes to us because they are being tormented or harassed and Tina was no exception. She was an exquisitely lovely young lady, tall and slender with shining golden hair. She easily could have passed for a model straight from the fashion runway. Although her beauty was breathtaking, many considered her a "scatterbrain."

When she first came to see us, it was hard for us to assign her the homework because she would not stop chattering. When she came the second time, her homework was not completed and we were surprised, because we had never encountered this type of behavior before. We patiently went over the assignment in detail one more time and felt that she understood everything. But when she came for her third appointment, once again she had not done her assignment.

We were beginning to get frustrated with her lack of progress in the deliverance sessions. We decided to have her work on her assignment right then and there, in our presence. We made this decision because we didn't think we could trust her to do it on her own. The Lord revealed to us that this beautiful young lady was bound by the strongest spirits of confusion, stupor, forgetfulness and mind binding that we had ever seen.

We began to pray deliverance over Tina and the anointing flowed very heavily. However, we felt like we were speaking to an empty head or running into a brick wall. She received some deliverance, but very little. Then all of a sudden, the Lord gave Claire discernment that Tina had *spirit guides*. We told her that the deliverance was not working because she had spirit guides and they were hindering the deliverance. We explained that she needed to renounce them verbally before we could proceed successfully.

Tina's reply to us was, "What are spirit guides?" We explained that whenever you get involved in meditation and invite someone or something to come inside you, what enters is called a spirit guide. Her eyes got really big and she exclaimed, "Oh, yes, now I remember! I practiced meditation back in college and I invited a little guy that looked like a leprechaun to enter. He wore green, had red hair, and his name was Henry." Then she cried out again, "There's another one, too. She's an Indian woman named Hiawatha and she has long, black, flowing hair."

Before Tina left the deliverance session, she had remembered two more spirit guides. What people don't realize is that these "spirit guides" they invite in are really evil demons. This practice is part of the New Age Movement that is sweeping the country and seducing the world today.

We instructed Tina to go home and renounce all the things that had come into her from the occult activity of her past. We set her up for another appointment and when she returned for that session, we began by breaking the ungodly soul ties between her and all these spirit guides. From that time on, everything went smoothly and she experienced deliverance and freedom! At last!

You need to understand that demons are rude guests! They do not leave until they are kicked out, and if they have a legal right to stay, they will *never* leave. After all, they have been invited in and given the authority to remain in residency.

INHERITED DEMONS

Although the following testimony did not come from a deliverance in our own ministry, we feel it is important to relate. The story was told to us by an individual whom we know personally.

The elderly woman, whom we will call Sarah, was short,

petite, and neatly dressed. She was obviously very intelligent and highly educated. Sarah was twenty-six when her mother died and it had been very traumatic for her. Much later in Sarah's life she found out that her father had viciously killed her mother with a cane.

Just weeks after the mother's funeral, Sarah was walking down a sidewalk when she heard someone call her name three times. "Sarah! Sarah! Sarah!" Sarah looked around and saw her mother walking toward her. Sarah ran but her mother chased her for four blocks, then disappeared. After this, Sarah's mother started appearing at the end of her bed each night and this continued for three months. Each night her mother said the same thing, "Honey, I am so cold; I want to come in."

Sarah started to emotionally "lose it" and her husband, who never saw anything, felt his wife was going crazy. Their marriage began to suffer and Sarah became more desperate each day. Finally, after three long months of absolute terror, one night she said to this apparition that looked like her mother, "Mother, just do whatever you have to do. I can't take this pleading anymore; you're driving me completely crazy!" As soon as the words were out of her mouth, Sarah began to freeze and she shook so violently that it scared her husband. Soon the shaking ceased and she never saw her "mother" again.

Immediately after this incident, Sarah's personality completely changed. She became like her mother in every way, including her appetite for certain foods. Sarah had always loved oatmeal, but her mother couldn't stand it. However, the morning after this encounter, Sarah found that she suddenly hated oatmeal, and even to this day, she cannot eat it.

The true story of Sarah is a perfect example of familiar spirits coming down through the inherited bloodline. Just remember this, dear reader. People die—but spirits don't!

You want to keep whatever godly that you have received from your ancestors. By the same token, you need to get rid of anything you may have received that is UNGODLY.

PASTORS DELIVERED

A church we attended had periodic training conferences for pastors, associate pastors, and leaders from across the nation. We were allowed to offer a teaching class on deliverance to those who were interested and some even gave up their lunch break to attend.

During the class we distributed a list of Stronghold Forces and all the demons that they have rule over. After carefully reading this list, one of the pastors told us that he had every one on the list. We could tell that this came as a shock to him—but not to us, as we have heard this comment before.

As the class continued, people began to ask if they could do a "self-deliverance." We explained that sometimes spirits are so deeply rooted that you really need some additional prayer power to help. Also, if you have a deceiving spirit, it will not let you know what demonic influences are present. Consequently, they unanimously decided to return that evening for a mass deliverance. This was going to be a FIRST for us, and we weren't sure how to proceed, but we knew that the Holy Spirit would take over, no matter what we had in mind or planned.

The evening flowed from beginning to end with great freedom. At one point, a problem arose with a demon, but a spontaneous group singing about the blood of Jesus put an end to that demon! The people bonded with such unity that whenever a demon would manifest, all of them would lay on hands and pray for the individual in bondage. It seemed like everything that *could* happen during a deliverance session *did*. Demons spoke through people, people got violent, some laughed and some cried. It was truly a "hands on" teaching—with life-changing results.

The following week we received a number of phone calls from people with reports that lives had been changed and they were walking in more freedom than they had ever dreamed possible. One pastor shared with us that when he preached his next sermon, he experienced more anointing than he had ever known before in his lifetime of ministry.

TORMENTED BY LUST

Many, many pastors from diverse denominations are controlled by demonic strongholds of lust and perversion and come to us for counsel. This is certainly an indication that satan will snare anyone, in any profession!

We had three pastors come to us in three weeks because of their obsession with lust, perversion and homosexuality. They absolutely hated what they were doing but had an undying drive that was just as pushy as a heroin addict.

These pastors, all truly devoted to God with a deep love for the Lord, had the doors of lust opened to them when they were small children. One pastor had looked at a lot of pornography and the other two men had been sexually molested.

A pastor came to us who was sexually active with many women other than his wife. He testified that as a child he had been introduced to extremely grotesque, perverted acts by his little friends—the sons of his pastor and head deacon.

Another pastor came to us but never mentioned any problems of homosexuality. However, as we began praying, a female voice spoke through him. We immediately knew what his problem was and called out the "feminine" personality of homosexuality.

If you are a pastor, priest, or evangelist, and are being tormented by spirits of lust or perversion, you need to know that you can be set free! Do not continue to live in bondage to these spirits. It is time to get TOTAL VICTORY IN YOUR LIFE!

THE OTHER SIDE OF THE COIN

Natalie, a young girl with jet black hair, sinful eyes, and a hard countenance, came to us because she was terrified! She had endured years of abuse and had been living an amoral, evil life. Recently she had experienced something that had her running scared—and she came to us for a quick fix!

A few nights before she came to us, she had been pinned to the floor by a demon and her eyes had been opened to the spirit world. The demon had actually scratched her face, neck and chest, and she was living in a state of panic and alarm.

We were happy to counsel her and speak truth to her, but we quickly discovered that she had no intention of becoming born again and turning her life over to Jesus Christ. She liked her wicked life and had turned cold to anything concerning God. It seemed like she had a heart of stone. She wanted to be free but she did not want to pay the price!

And even as they did not like to retain God in their knowledge, God gave them over to a reprobate mind, to do those things which are not convenient. (Rom. 1:28)

We will not pray deliverance for anyone unless they are willing to give their life completely to Jesus. By doing so, we could do them more harm than good. Without the power of God in your life, you have no way of keeping the deliverance. Natalie made it very clear that she absolutely was not interested in anything that had to do with God, the Bible, church, or Jesus. Sadly, she went away and we never heard from her again. We still grieve over Natalie and pray for her every day!

PAUL'S UNGODLY SOUL TIE

One evening Claire and I attended a powerful service at

Carpenter's Home Church in Lakeland, Florida, conducted by Rodney Howard-Browne. Driving home after service, we were still in the afterglow of the anointing of the Holy Spirit, when I heard a voice in my spirit say, "You need to break the ungodly soul tie between you and your father." I quickly thought to myself, "That's not necessary." My father was a godly man, a minister of the gospel for over forty years, and we had a healthy relationship. A few moments passed and then the same voice said, "If you break the ungodly soul tie between you and your father, I will heal your sinus problem right now."

All my life I had fought a severe sinus problem that caused an irritating drainage in the back of my throat. I was on antibiotics or antihistamines almost constantly. I had asked God to heal me and had been prayed for many times, but nothing ever happened.

My father had fought the same battle; his sinuses were so bad that he always preached with the microphone in one hand and a handkerchief in the other. His father (my grandfather) had died at a relatively early age from pneumonia. We have learned that spirits of infirmity are also familiar spirits that come from generational curses.

As we drove down the freeway, I shared with Claire what God had just said to me, and she immediately reached into her purse and brought out the anointing oil. When God says NOW, there is not a second to waste. We began to pray and before I knew what happened, Claire anointed me with oil. I felt an urgency to really get down to business in prayer, so my voice became loud and stern, and I spoke these words with authority, "I break the ungodly soul tie between me and my father and his ancestors, and between my father and me. Demon, I command you to leave, in the Name of Jesus." Then I put what we call a "Jesus bloodline" between my father and me and continued praying with God-given authority and power. "**Satan, you and your kingdom cannot cross this Jesus bloodline. You or any of your kingdom**

will never cross this bloodline again. Spirit of infirmity and sinus trouble, I command you to leave me NOW in the Name of Jesus."

Suddenly I felt something leave through my fingertips, as well as through the top of my head. Within forty-five seconds, my lifelong battle was finally over—my sinuses completely dried up and have remained healthy ever since.

There was a generational curse that had to be broken before I could receive my healing. The spirit of infirmity had to go after the ungodly soul tie was broken and the spirit was commanded to leave. It had to leave—it had no choice but to go. You see, it had lost its legal right to be there! Thank God for the blood of the Lamb and the fact that He took the curse for us at Calvary!

I remember that a lady in our church was scheduled for serious surgery and she was given only a fifty-fifty chance to survive. She had been receiving prayer for her problem for the past ten years and nothing had happened. However, after we broke the ungodly soul ties and cast out a spirit of infirmity, she received her healing! She was able to cancel the surgery, after all. Praise the Lord! All glory to God!

God is so wonderful. He has given us all we would ever need to be victorious over the enemy. We have personally learned things from the Holy Spirit that only God could have revealed to us. He has revealed these things to us in order that individuals can be set free!

DEMONS VISITED OUR BEDROOM—CLAIRE

A pastor asked us to meet him in his office one evening because he wanted us to meet some people. When we arrived, the pastor introduced us to a very lovely young couple who had the most frightened looks on their faces we had ever seen. Even though the couple did not attend this pastor's church, they had come to him in total desperation, hoping that he could help them.

Earlier that morning, while still asleep, this young wife had been attacked by two demons that awakened her by choking her. She saw them plainly and really thought she was going to die. Her husband was horrified and mystified, and thought his wife had gone completely mad. Of course, he didn't know how to handle the situation, but his wife ran out of the house, jumped in the car, and drove directly to this pastor's house—at five o'clock in the morning!

We talked with this couple for a while, then scheduled them for an appointment, giving them our business card, telling them to call if they needed us before the appointment. At two o'clock that very morning, she called for prayer and Paul prayed for her. He bound up the spirits that were harassing her and commanded them to leave her alone, in Jesus' Name.

The next morning, Paul told me of an unusual experience he had during the night, one he had never had before. After praying for this young woman, while he was trying to go back to sleep, a demon came into our bedroom, got on top of Paul's back, and lifted up his arm.

"Were you scared?" I asked Paul.

He replied, "No, of course not. I didn't even open my eyes. I just brushed it off, like you would brush off a cat." But then he went on, "You're not going to believe this, but as soon as that demon left, another one came and did exactly the same thing." Paul just commanded that demon to leave in the Name of Jesus, like he had the other one.

After Paul shared this with me, he asked, "Why did you sit up in bed right after this happened?" Suddenly I remembered what had happened and I shouted, "I KNOW THEIR NAMES!" I ran to where I had written two names on a pad of paper.

I remembered that I had been asleep but was awakened suddenly by something and I sat up in bed and immediately reached for the pad of paper and pencil I always keep by my bed. I knew in my spirit that I knew the names of the two demons that had been attacking this woman: ANDABON and ANGRULF. I wrote them phonetically because they were strange words to me.

The pastor that had introduced this couple to us told us later that these demons also came into his bedroom the night they visited us, during the same hour.

When we met this young woman at her deliverance session, I told her that when we pray, we might use some strange names during the session. When I mentioned the first name, she shot out of the chair like she had been plugged into a 220 electrical socket! Her eyes bulged and got as big as saucers. Then she finally calmed down and I mentioned the second name. She did a repeat performance! We then knew that the same demons that had been tormenting her had visited our bedroom—and we had their names!

During her deliverance session, we found that she had strong spirits of fear, bondage, heaviness, and rejection. But she was completely set free in the Name of Jesus! Since that time these young people have grown in the Lord and are serving Him in a marvelous way.

You may be a child of God but you can still have satan and his kingdom harassing you! That's why it is vital that you know the truth about your authority in the Name of Jesus.

EX-WITCH

In our ministry we have seen many former witches. They are more serious about being set free than the average person, because they KNOW what it is to walk on the dark side. They also know for certain that there is only one way to break away from witchcraft and that is through JESUS!

An ex-witch recently told us that every time she had sexual activity with a man, she would put fifteen to twenty demons in him. She knew that she had the legal right to do this—and she enjoyed it. She made the comment that when these men came to see her, they went home with a whole lot more than they bargained for. I am sure none of these men ever dreamed that she was a practicing witch, and the last thing on their minds or in their wildest nightmares would be that she was putting demons into them.

Now that this woman is born again, she feels remorseful about having done this. She is the sweetest, most soft-spoken lady you would ever hope to meet.

What? Know ye not that he which is joined to an harlot is one body? For two, saith he, shall be one flesh. (I Cor. 6:16)

DEMONS WERE PART OF HIS HOUSEHOLD

Andy was an athletic high school student, muscular and handsome with curly brown hair. Upon meeting this young man, we immediately discerned that he was under great demonic oppression. The demons would get especially angry when he was close to the anointing, as when he attended a church service where the power of God was flowing.

He had given his heart to the Lord and truly wanted to live completely for Christ, but these demonic strongholds held him back. He knew he needed help, so he came to us. His mother was into occult practices and, in fact, had dedicated a room in their home to satan. Strange things happened in that room and Andy told us that when he entered it, a power like electricity flowed through his body.

Andy knew that four demons lived in his house and he knew them well. He told us their names and described how they dressed. Omar was a swordsman; Nye was a martial arts expert; Omdropolis was strong, old, wise, and had a beard; and Caisha dressed in a warrior's outfit.

One day Andy visited the home of a very important warlock; the warlock was actually in charge of a large section of the entire United States. (We had another person give us identical information about this same warlock—and these individuals had never met or even heard of each other.)

On Andy's day to be prayed for, he was late and he actually had to walk several miles in the heat of the day to make his appointment. But he was very determined to be set free!

In our session with Andy, we broke all the ungodly soul ties between him and the demons living in his house. During this prayer, he literally went crazy and power rose up in him like a gorilla. The demons were enraged, but one by one we called them out by name. Satan's kingdom loses and Christ wins, because He won the victory on the cross two thousand years ago. All we have to do is BELIEVE IT AND USE THE AUTHORITY HE HAS GIVEN TO US.

One of satan's best tools in keeping Christians bound is to keep them from realizing the authority they have within themselves through Jesus Christ. Satan knows that when we realize that the God who created him and his kingdom now lives in us, and we get hold of the truth that satan has to bow to that authority, he (satan) is under our feet!

Andy was gloriously delivered that day because he took hold of the wonderful truth of his victory in Jesus Christ!

ROOTS CURSE—CLAIRE

Zoë, a beautiful young woman, always looked nervous and during the deliverance session, she was obviously uneasy. Her hands were shaking and her eyes darted around the room. In our dealings with her, we had not discovered any unforgiveness, unrenounced occult activity, or unconfessed sin in her life. Yet, she was attacked daily by unseen powers that left her with bites on her skin, feelings of intense heat, failures in her work and unrealistic feelings of rejection from those around her. Also, her body emitted a strange, foul odor.

After several sessions, we realized that a curse of some kind was affecting Zoë. Her mother-in-law was very active in a religion called "roots." This religion is located predominantly in southern states and its adherents cast spells, perform voodoo, and practice other activities related to witchcraft. For instance, they put cursed ingredients in your food, or try to get hold of personal items, such as hair from your comb, to use in occult ceremonies.

Just as with all witchcraft and occult activities, roots is allowed to work by a spirit of fear. Zoë had spent some time at the home of her mother-in-law and since she knew what the woman was involved in, she took great pains to avoid any possible connection with the practices and beliefs. For instance, knowing that she could be cursed through the food, she ate all her meals at the local McDonald's. Also, she made sure that she didn't leave any hair on her pillow or in her comb. She was meticulous in tidying up on the counters and on the floor, in case any of her hair had fallen.

We were able to pinpoint that all Zoë's problems began after the final visit to her mother-in-law's house, in spite of all her precautions. She was knowledgeable enough to know that satan would leave her when she prayed and praised, so when she felt an attack coming on, that is what she would do.

By the time Zoë came to see us, she was desperate! She had been to see medical doctors because of sharp, razor-like pains in her pelvic area and sometimes she felt like a knife was stabbing her, followed by an intense heat. She also had unexplained bites appear on her legs. She felt sure the symptoms were physical in origin, but after undergoing numerous tests, nothing physically wrong could be found.

This is the condition Zoë was in when she came to see us. When we got discernment on what was tormenting her, we prayed deliverance for her. Immediately a demon began to manifest. She put her hands together as in prayer, bowed her head, then began to move her head up and down rapidly. Her face became distorted, took on a strange, Oriental appearance with slanted eyes, and she began to chant in an "unknown tongue." We knew we were onto something, but this was our first experience of breaking curses. The Holy Spirit guided us in taking control in prayer and the curse was finally broken!

Zoë experienced a great deal of relief but some of the problems persisted. We scheduled several additional sessions with her and felt we should break any ungodly soul ties with her relatives and ancestors. When we prayed this way, the demons went crazy. Her face contorted so badly that she did not even look human and, as we mentioned, she was a very beautiful young woman. Her lips rolled up and turned inside out. Her mouth made a big ring and looked like a doughnut. Her eyes were bulging out of her head and all her facial features seemed sort of loosened up and just swayed back and forth, first in a clockwise, then a counter-clockwise motion.

We kept praying for Zoë and when we came against any curses her mother-in-law had put on her and spoke the woman's name, the demons glared at us in fury.

On one occasion, Zoë manifested like a snake, hissing as she stuck out her tongue, so we came against any fiery serpent curse. She told us after her deliverance that she kept seeing a huge snake right up in her face.

Several times Zoë manifested by stooping over and squinting her eyes at us. After she was free, she told us that she had felt like she was a really old person during the prayers. At one point, we were both down on the floor with her and we were so exhausted physically that we just sat. Paul began singing about the BLOOD OF JESUS and I joined in (even though my singing is very bad). As we sang, the demons kept leaving on their own, without our help.

Finally, Zoë began to laugh. I got a bit agitated and disgusted because I though the demons were laughing at my singing, but then I realized the laughter was coming from Zoë because she was experiencing great freedom and joy! The blood of Jesus has all power over the enemy. Just applying the Word even when you are totally physically exhausted *works*!

Zoë was set free! But it took several long and difficult sessions. Even though she had been born again and was free of sin, leading a clean and holy life, these curses evidently still had a legal right to have an effect on her because of the *fear she had of the curses.* When Zoë was a small child, her mother had taught her to stay away from all "roots" people, not to eat their food or associate with them in any way. Although her mother meant to protect her, she had opened a door to allow fear in Zoë's life. We learned from this experience that the curse cannot hurt you (if you are a Christian), but the FEAR of the curse can be deadly.

Poor, dear Zoë had been suffering intense symptoms for five years because of this attack of satan and medical doctors were not able to diagnose her problems. If you are suffering from an illness that doctors cannot explain, the problem may be spiritual in nature. If that is the case, you may never be healed by natural means. It will probably take a spiritual deliverance!

DELIVERANCE MINISTER SET FREE—CLAIRE

When we began our ministry, our only exposure to deliverance had been through a couple from another part of the state who was involved in a deliverance ministry. We had been amazed at the wife's keen discernment of spirits.

Later, when we were thrust into the deliverance ministry, the Lord gave us complete wisdom and knowledge about how to put it together. We knew we were not smart enough to do it by our own knowledge, so we relied totally on Him. The Lord *must* give the discernment and power, because without Him we can not do it!

We had been involved with deliverance ministry for a couple of years and had not seen this couple during that time. However, they came to visit us and I invited the wife to accompany me to a retreat for women. During the retreat, five people approached me asking to be put on our waiting list for deliverance. I told the first person that I would be glad to pray for her after the service the next evening. We met and I went over everything that Paul and I normally covered during the first and second appointments.

My friend who went with me to the retreat (I'll call her Cathy) sat in the meeting with me and seemed astounded by all the information I went through. "Claire, I need this myself! You have to pray for me!" Here was a woman actively involved in powerful ministry asking me to pray for her!

A little while later, Paul and I did pray for Cathy, and she knew what she was talking about when she said she needed prayer. She needed to be set free from a lot of demonic activity in her own life.

You may ask, how can a person successfully pray deliverance for others and have demon strongholds herself? It is because we are calling out demonic spirits with our "spirit man." In our book entitled *THIS MEANS WAR*, you will find an in-depth teaching explaining that demonic activity is in your "soulish" area, and other related topics.

If you were performing deliverance in your flesh (soulish part), the demons would beat up on you. You are no match for a demon, but JESUS IS! And Jesus is inside your *spirit* man. The God that lives in you has all power, all authority, over demons and even satan himself. Jesus won the battle when He died and rose again, and now all the demonic kingdom has to bow to the AUTHORITY OF JESUS CHRIST that resides in you.

We prayed for our friend, Cathy, and she immediately began to manifest demonic spirits. When Paul called out any personality to leave that wasn't the "born again" Cathy, a demon immediately spoke through her, saying, "Don't make me go. I'll be good—I'll be good!"

There were at least two stronghold demons that tried to kill her. For the first time in our ministry, I got concerned. Cathy was choking and couldn't seem to stop. I hurriedly poured anointing oil on my hands—through the Lord's discernment—and rushed back to her side. I put my hands on her throat and commanded the demon not to hurt her. It left—but it really showed off on the way out.

Normally when we break ungodly soul ties, nothing much happens. But in Cathy's case, the devils began to violently choke her for some reason. However, there is a victorious end to this story! Cathy was gloriously set free and immediately went back to her church and shared her testimony of deliverance with all her friends. They were so excited that they wanted to get on our waiting list. I guess they felt that if it worked for Cathy, it would work for them, too!

This is a perfect example of how we all need to get rid of things that have happened in our life before we were born again. These are the things that opened the doorway to satan and his kingdom.

WHICH ONE WAS SHE?—CLAIRE

Karen, a red-haired beauty with a flawless complexion, had a countenance shadowed by sadness. One look into her deep blue eyes betrayed her otherwise "perfect" life. She and her handsome young husband had an angelic, lovely baby and seemingly all the things in life one could ever hope for. Yet—that pervasive sadness hovered around her and seemed to linger even after she had left the room.

Paul commented that there must be something dreadfully wrong in her life and I agreed. She finally came to us for counseling and after several sessions, we decided she definitely needed prayer for deliverance. We were in for quite a surprise! This was our first experience with such extreme manifestations during prayer. We called out several spirits, but when Paul commanded the spirit of PRIDE to come out, by the authority of the blood and in the Name of Jesus, Karen straightened up in her chair. She sat very tall and straight, and looked down her nose at us. She began screaming in a loud voice, "NO! NO! NO! I will not come out!"

Demons have no choice about whether or not to come out, because they all *have to come out*. When a person does the homework and truly desires deliverance, the demons leave.

Next, we addressed the spirit of slumber, or stupor, and Karen suddenly "passed out" for about five or ten minutes.

At different times during the deliverance, demons would speak through her and physically fight us with the strength of a man. When Paul called out specific demons, Karen screamed "NO! NO!" and shook her head so violently that her hair accessories flew around the room. The demeanor of this refined, gentle young lady changed and she became like a wild woman. Even though she was quite petite, she almost raised Paul off the floor in her struggles. We stayed with her, spent a lot of time and effort, covered all the bases, and finally she was gloriously set free!

Then the most shocking thing happened! The very next week, Karen went straight downhill and became so oppressed that by Saturday she was experiencing feelings of murder. We met with her that afternoon and she looked terrible when she came in.

"I feel like I'm two different people," Karen told us. We explored this and found that, in fact, there were *twenty-six* distinct personalities present in her body. During the first deliverance session, an *imposter personality* had shown up but the *real* Karen showed up the second time. As we prayed, each of the twenty-six personalities manifested many times, and we all got physically exhausted. But we assured Karen we were committed to staying with her until she was *completely free*, and it took a long time.

At one point Paul called out a spirit of self-pity and she began to cry and sob like a baby; she sounded like her heart would break. I found myself feeling sorry for her and went over and hugged her. In a flash I realized that I was being manipulated by a demon! I quickly backed off and resumed my spiritual warfare. Beware! Demons can really suck you in to their games and deceit if you are not careful! I learned a lot from that experience and now I keep a special guard up against demonic power. The Holy Spirit has been able to help many people as a result of these experiences that day with Karen.

Actually, we learned several valuable things about demonic activity during the sessions with Karen. *Demons will try to outsmart you!* When you are calling out a particular demon, it may manifest by stiffening up, resisting, and screaming. Then it will act like it is coming out and the person will go completely limp and seem very relieved. Then when we ask the person if the demon has left, the person will agree that it is gone. However, this could be deception. We have found that God will give us supernatural discernment if it is still there. This happens almost every time we call out a spirit of lying and deception. Only the Holy Spirit can give this discernment and reveal to you a demon's tricks.

Karen also had a condemning spirit that would speak out through her during deliverance and say, "Karen is dumb! She is *so dumb!*" She had been cursed with migraine headaches that caused "lights" to go off in her head. These lights left when we called out a spirit of addiction. We found that there was an ungodly soul tie between Karen and her grandmother that had to be broken, because the demon looked at us and snarled, "I killed her grandmother and I am going to kill her, too!" Later, Karen told us that her grandmother had died as the result of a brain hemorrhage.

After Karen's deliverance, her entire countenance changed. Today she is happy, bright-eyed, smiling and has the look of an overcoming Christian rather than someone in constant defeat.

The experience with Karen taught us to always begin a deliverance session by casting out all multi-personalities that are not the "born again" personality. This approach in spiritual warfare during deliverance saves a lot of time for the person praying deliverance and causes the person seeking deliverance to be completely set free. If a multi-personality comes to the deliverance session and has taken over the true personality, you won't get anywhere. You must get the true personality back in control before the deliverance can take place.

SEX WITH A DEMON

Sarah, a fashionable, intelligent, attractive young woman, was a gifted artist. She was very friendly and, in spite of her extreme talent, she appeared to be humble.

She came to us at the very start of our deliverance ministry and, frankly, we were trying to be cool. We told her to feel free to confide completely in us because we would not be shocked and would not betray her confidence. Well, we weren't quite prepared for what she told us that day.

When Sarah began telling us about having sex with a demon, we just listened as though we knew all about that kind of stuff. Actually, at that point we were totally clueless about sexual activity with demons. When she left the room for a moment, we almost fell off our chairs! We looked at each other in shock and disbelief, but since then we have had several women tell us that they were having sexual relations with demons.

Sarah was molested constantly by her father when she was a child and she had a little "imaginary friend" who became very real to her and visited her every night. When she reached puberty, her "friend" began having sexual relations with her and this lasted for many years. Actually, even when we saw Sarah, the "friend" was still very real in her life. This "friend" was a demon spirit and would not leave until we broke an ungodly soul tie between the two of them. After the day of deliverance, Sarah never saw him again.

When Sarah had a child of her own, she had to overcome strong temptations to molest her baby. The temptations came every day and she struggled to resist. There was a generational curse of lust and child molestation that had entered when her father molested her. Even though she still struggled with a spirit of lust, she was determined not to touch her own child, and she succeeded in this area. This generational curse was not completely broken until the day of the deliverance.

Sarah's deliverance was marvelous and today she shares her complete testimony with many.

SPIRIT OF FEAR

Peggy had been delivered from a strong spirit of fear in our deliverance program and she had walked in victory. However, she had a test of her faith and trust a few months after her deliverance.

Peggy was scheduled for major surgery on the back of her neck and in order to reach the area, the surgeon had to cut into the front of her throat. The evening before she was to have surgery, she went to church, so she had thoroughly prepared her spirit. However, as she was lying in her hospital bed awaiting surgery, she could feel a spirit of fear come down upon her. She said it was so real that she felt she could almost touch it, and she pulled the blanket up over her head and cowered in the bed.

Peggy knew that the fear would engulf her in seconds if she didn't do something. As soon as she made up her mind to fight, the Holy Spirit came upon her, she threw back the covers, and almost shouted, "Fear, I know who you are—you know who I am—and you know the God I serve. *Now, fear, get out of my face!"* And, of course, the spirit of fear left her in a flash!

After deliverance, it is vital to recognize the enemy and his tactics. We need to become offensive soldiers instead of defensive. Satan knows how to push your buttons but you need to recognize the power within you to fight back in the spirit.

OCCULT RITUAL

Anna was an average looking, middle-aged housewife from our area. She wore her long, straight, brown hair pulled to the back of her head, and she seemed extremely shy and retiring. When she first came to see us, she was confused, disoriented, full of fear, and distrustful.

When we tried to explore her past, she was unclear and was able to provide us with only bits and pieces of information. Before we begin a counseling session, we pray over each other and over the room. There is always a heavy anointing in the room. We dispatch mighty warring angels to encamp around the room and I believe Anna was able to recall exactly what we needed to know because of this.

At first, her recollections were hazy and sketchy and the only thing she could remember before the age of twelve was having a lot of pornography in her home. She thought that perhaps she and her brother had acted out some of the sex scenes. In fact, as she continued to share, and we put the pieces together, we were certain that, in fact, this had happened.

Twelve years before Anna came to see us, her mother had set up a double date for the two of them and they were to meet their dates at a restaurant. Anna and her mother drove to the restaurant together, met their dates, ate dinner and had a rather uneventful time. Then Anna's date persuaded her to go with him to his place to sample some homemade wine he had made. Her mother and her date stayed at the restaurant.

Anna's date gave her some wine and at the first taste, her head seemed to get as heavy as a cement block and events followed that are very confused in her mind. He lived on a farm and took her to the basement, where he had a deer. She remembers that suddenly the room was full of people, all of them nude (including her), but then she remembers lying on a table with a sheet covering her body and a large fan blowing over her head. The details and memories were very sketchy, but we were beginning to get the impression of occult rituals and activities. Anna is certain that she saw her family doctor in the crowd in the basement that night.

During the twelve years between that double date and the time Anna saw us, she got flashbacks of some of the events. She would ask her mother questions about what really happened that night, but her mother denied that they had even gone on a double date. However, after a time, she did admit that the double date had occurred. Anna had the same questions over and over and finally her mother screamed at her, "Don't ask me any more questions! Are you trying to GET ME KILLED?"

We had several sessions with Anna and by the final deliverance session, she realized that she might have been used in some kind of occult ritual. However, regardless of what happened, she knew she needed to forgive everyone involved and not hold any judgment against them. Instead, she needed to get mad at the satanic influence behind the events.

Many times when you realize how much satan has stolen from you, you get angry enough at his influence to be ready for a great deliverance!

Anna is now free of all demonic ties. We hear from her once in a while and she always has good reports of continuing victory.

51

MENTAL INSTITUTION ESCAPE—CLAIRE

Jill, a tiny, quiet woman in her early thirties, called us from an air force base and requested our help. The military wanted to send her to a mental hospital for observation because she had been having bouts of fainting. She indicated that this had started right after she returned home from her grandmother's funeral.

"Did your grandmother have a problem with passing out?" we asked her.

"Well, yes, she passed out all the time."

We found that there had been a strong bond between the two of them and even though our schedule was extremely busy and we had a long waiting list, we felt an urgency to make time for her and her husband right away.

When I greeted the two of them in the waiting room, she was incoherent and uncommunicative. When we asked her questions, she sat and stared into space, never responding. Her husband did all the talking, and answered questions for her. It was really sad to see her in such a state.

Both Paul and I discerned that her condition related to her grandmother's death. I explained to Jill that when people die, the demons that are in them don't die and they want to stay in the same bloodline. In this case, because of her close emotional tie with her grandmother, the spirits simply transferred over to her when her grandmother died. In fact, there seemed to be an ungodly soul tie and possibly this opened the doors that gave them a legal right to transfer.

As soon as Jill heard this, she came to herself, looked at her husband in amazement, and said, "You know, they are absolutely correct! This really makes sense to me. Oh, thank God, I know now that I'm not crazy!"

We assured both Jill and her husband that she could be set free and we gave them homework to do. Before they left, however, Jill related another interesting story to us. It seems that she had very unpleasant, even horrifying, memories of Christmas. Her mother always had a "nervous breakdown" during the holiday season and spent the entire time away in a hospital.

We were seeing Jill during the Christmas season and one day we received a telephone call informing us that she had been rushed to a mental facility. We hurried to the facility and found her to be very confused, nervous, and acting strangely. She kept going in and out of reality and when we tried to pray with her, she tried to get away from us. Finally, she jumped up and left the room, so we gave up and went home. Her husband later told us that she had to be restrained by hospital workers during the night because she was doing some very weird things. We realized that the demons were just acting up because they knew they were going to lose their home.

The following day we visited Jill at the mental facility and found her sedated. We anointed the room with oil, prayed over her, and bound up each demon by specific name. Every time we called out the demon's name, Jill's body would jerk, so we knew that things were taking place in the spirit realm. Paul and I were strongly anointed and we felt that the Lord allowed us to pray for her while she was sedated so that she would offer no resistance. At this time we did not cast out the demons, we merely bound them up and made plans to return a week later for a complete deliverance session.

When Jill woke up, she was in her right mind! The demons had been bound and she was able to get dressed, wash her hair, and function normally. She never had to have any more medication and she seemed so bright and healthy that the other patients at the facility thought she was a staff member.

The day of her deliverance session came and since we had never prayed deliverance for anyone on satan's turf before, we came prepared! As we entered the building, we bound up every evil spirit that could possibly be in control of the hospital and we bound up satan and his kingdom from being active in any way, shape or form.

We entered the hospital at three o'clock in the afternoon and Jill told us that someone was scheduled to come in to check on her at five o'clock. Paul stationed an angel at the door so no one could come in until we were completely finished. And he also commanded the demons *not* to make one sound.

When we began to pray, Jill became very violent and her strength was surprising for one with such a dainty, delicate frame. At one point, when Paul called out a spirit of insanity, she went for his throat! The demon spoke through her (although not loudly), shaking her head back and forth and sideways. "I am not leaving! I have my orders!" Regardless of what the demon said, we knew it would have to leave simply because it had no choice in the matter!

The demons in Jill were so strong that they pushed her chair all around the room—but *they never made a sound*! She had multiple personalities, familiar spirits, and many other powerful spirits, but she was completely set free that day!

The military had scheduled Jill to be flown out to a military hospital in a neighboring state two days later. At that hospital they did the routine observational study and exams on her. Her doctor was puzzled and asked her why she was there. "Someone has made a terrible mistake. There is nothing wrong with you. Why were you sent here?" Jill had scored better on the tests than he did himself, so he sent her home immediately.

Paul and I are now good friends with Jill and her husband and we are thrilled to see that she is one of the happiest women you will ever meet. We love and respect this couple and rejoice with them that the Lord proved Himself in such a mighty way in their lives.

THE VOICES WON'T STOP!

Amy was only in her late twenties and her body was in great shape because she was a health fitness instructor, but her face looked at least forty! Torment was painted across her face, she was wrinkled, and her eyes were sunken in their sockets. It was almost impossible to hold her attention and even though she would look at you, her eyes had a faraway, glazed appearance.

Amy was referred to us by an employee of a local television station who knew we did deliverance. She had been tormented by voices in her head for a long time. The voices were varied and constant, causing her many sleepless night and terror-filled days. The terror was unrelenting.

In talking with Amy, we discovered that she had dated a doctor who was into satanism and he had forced her to do some really weird things. The voices had started during that time and had not ever gone away.

Amy was wonderfully delivered after we broke the spirit of fear, any ungodly soul ties between her and the doctor, and a curse which had been put on her.

This deliverance clearly points out the importance of using discretion in our friendships and other relationships.

FOUL ODOR

Eight years before we met her, Erica had been in prison for child abuse. Her son was taken from her and she never saw him again. Now she was a middle-aged woman, happily married and the mother of another child.

Erica's great personality and outward beauty were very appealing, but appearances are deceptive. She actually was filled with pain, guilt, and shame because of her past, and she was being heavily oppressed by satan.

Even though Erica loved God and had a deep hunger to

know Him better, she knew where her inward oppression came from and she wanted to be set free. Her desire to serve God included a hope to help others get freed from bondage, but she knew she could not do this if she herself was bound.

Erica made a list of all the people she had bitterness and unforgiveness toward. Then she made a deliberate choice to forgive them! Further, she renounced all occult activities and broke all ungodly soul ties. When she burned the list of names and activities (this is part of the homework we assign), a foul smell resembling rotten eggs filled her house. It was intense and so horrid that she and a Christian friend commanded the odor to leave, in the Name of Jesus! The smell immediately left the house.

When we prayed for her, it seemed like demons came from everywhere. She had opened a lot of doors for satan and his kingdom to come in, and now Jesus was kicking them out. We also smelled a terrible stench when we prayed, and she spit up some unpleasantly foul-smelling, whitish liquid. However, the end of this story is that Erica was gloriously set free that very day! It was a struggle, but it was fruitful!

A couple of weeks after Erica's deliverance a woman phoned her and told her she was now the mother of the little son Erica had lost. She told Erica that she was a Christian and she wanted to grant Erica visitation rights to see her child. Erica was overjoyed and overwhelmed! She met the parents who were raising the boy and they immediately bonded through the Holy Spirit. Her life will never be the same!

HULK MAN—CLAIRE

George, an ordinary looking, 23-year-old man, came to us for deliverance. He was a polite, friendly young man, but his face looked hard, and old far beyond his years. He sat in a chair in front of Paul, and I was behind George with my hands on his shoulders. Paul told George to look him in the eyes, keep silent, and WILL the demons to go as they were being called out. Paul also instructed him that if he felt like coughing, sneezing, crying, yawning or responding in any other way, just to go ahead and do it. "Do not hold anything back," Paul said.

I heard Paul call out the spirit of anger and immediately George let out a loud, bloodcurdling GROWL. I looked at George and his appearance had absolutely changed. As he continued to growl, he puffed up like a frog—it was as if someone was blowing him up like a balloon. He looked like his clothes were going to split and be torn from his body. It reminded me of an old television show called "The Incredible Hulk" in which an ordinary man metamorphosed into a large, "hulking" character. George's appearance was truly bizarre!

We were brand new in deliverance ministry and since I had never seen anything like this, I had no idea what to do. He was exhibiting superhuman strength and I knew we could not hold him down. On impulse, I ran and found one of the pastors and he helped us hold George down.

Even though it was challenging and we were charting new areas, God was true to His Word and George was delivered (although a lot of noise was involved). Our pastor told us later that he was in a telephone conversation and the person on the other end of the line asked what all the growling and screaming was about. Our pastor's study was down a long hallway, across a reception area, and three more offices removed from where we were. And, further, the doors to all the offices were closed. But the Hulk Man screamed so loudly that it scared everyone in the 80,000 square-foot building.

We are happy to report that George walked out of that office that day a new person!

It's good for you to know that whenever the anger demons take over a person, they want to fight. We didn't know this until after we prayed for George, but if you try to hold a person down during deliverance, the demons love it; it "feeds" them and gives them more strength. The thing to do is just back off physically and simply command the demons to leave, walking in our authority in the Name of Jesus, and stay out of the human realm altogether.

TRANSFORMED BEFORE OUR EYES

We have witnessed many, many dramatic, even bizarre, things in our ministry up to this point, but none can compare with the dramatic, instantaneous change we saw in Susan. What Almighty God did for Susan still amazes us! And makes us so glad to be on the team of a God Who is so merciful and good.

A pastor's wife asked us to meet with Susan and our first visit with her was so intense and sensational that we never expected her to show up for a second appointment.

First appointments are designed as a time of getting acquainted; we visit, explain our ministry, then give a homework assignment to be completed by the next session. During Susan's first session, as we explained our ministry and the program, she began to manifest. The whites of her eyes turned as red as blood and she stared right through us. Frankly, it was like looking right into the eyes of the devil. She slid out of her chair and started crawling around on the floor, acting and barking like a dog!

Susan was not a small lady, yet she crawled under a chair, then right on through the legs of the chair, a feat that would have been impossible for her to do in the natural. She crawled to a corner of the room and assumed the fetal position. Suddenly, she reared up with the force of a stallion and started bellowing. She ran out of the room, almost tearing the door off its hinges, screaming, roaring all the way. She ran past everyone in the lobby area and found another corner, where she crouched down, whimpering.

Paul and I pursued her, of course, but when we got close to her, she strongly resisted us, running to another location. This went on for some time, but we finally got her back in the proper room. By this time, we did not know what to think. We certainly didn't think she would return for another visit, but we gave her the homework assignment, anyway. Part of our reason for thinking she would not return was because we did not think she had understood anything we had told her.

Surprise! Susan did come back for a second appointment and she came with a firm determination to defeat the devil in her life! We found out that she was carrying a lot of pain from physical, mental, emotional and spiritual abuse in her life. She had gone to a former pastor for counsel, but he had seduced her and held her in sexual bondage by twisting the Word of God for his purposes. She had been in a mental institution twice and she feared that she was on the verge of going back. But what impressed us was her determination to overcome all her problems. Demons had tormented her long enough and *now she was ready to fight back.*

In spite of her resolve, when Susan showed up on the day for deliverance, she was obviously in a nervous state, wringing her hands and fretting. Paul immediately, quietly said, "You nervous spirit, STOP in the Name of Jesus!" Susan's hands went to her sides and she settled right down. We pray over the anointing oil, believing that it truly is a symbol of the Holy Spirit and the blood of Jesus. Paul always anoints his own hands, and it is his practice to take a person by the hands when he prays for deliverance. The demons were afraid of Paul's hands because of the anointing oil. Demons tremble and are scared of the blood of Jesus because that is what defeated them. But when Paul tried to take Susan's hands, she refused. "NO! NO! Absolutely not!"

The demons were extremely upset over losing their home and Susan manifested violently, showing great strength and outrage. She literally tried to tear up the pastor's office (where we were meeting that day) and then the demon reached for Paul's throat, but I grabbed Susan's hand, prying it away.

The demons of fear and rejection put up quite a fight that day, and they were strong and tough. But after those demons left, Susan ended up on the floor, and smiled up at us. "What a trip!" she exclaimed.

Susan jumped up from where she had been lying and ran back to her chair. "Come on! Let's go for the next one!" She put her hands out for Paul to pray and was an altogether different person. We sat in total amazement! Susan felt the power and reality of her deliverance and she was so excited. She wanted to be rid of the spirits that had put her in the mental institution, so we prayed some more.

At the end of the deliverance session, Susan looked like a new person. Not only was her countenance changed, but she acted totally different, too. We see Susan quite often and can attest to the veracity of her deliverance. We still marvel at what Jesus did!

STRONG BUDDHA TIES

Keisha was a slightly built, dark-eyed, East Indian young woman. Her black hair hung far down her back and her deep-set eyes had dark circles around them, seeming even darker because of her olive complexion. One side of her nose had been pierced and bejeweled, adding to her striking appearance.

For many years, Keisha's brother had sexually abused her but she didn't have the courage to tell her parents until she was a teenager. Her father slapped her and told her never to mention such a thing again. In India, such things are closely guarded secrets because of fear of family humiliation.

Keisha was able to leave her homeland, and the brother who had abused her told her never to return. Keisha did not know it, but she was filled with tremendously strong spirits of rejection, lust, and timidity. This was coupled with a lot of occult activity in her background.

Keisha was taught to worship Buddha when she was growing up and she spent many nights with her little girlfriend who lived at a Buddhist temple where her father was a priest. After she came to America, Keisha learned about Jesus and completely gave her life over to him. Her greatest desire was to serve Him fully and faithfully.

When we prayed deliverance for Keisha, we had a very tough time because the demons kept attacking her body. She would scream so loudly that we thought she was going to pass out. She would grab her side and back over and over, as though she was in great pain. After the demon exited, she told us that it felt like she was being shot, with the bullet entering her back and exiting her side. We have found that this is a common experience during deliverance.

As we have said, demons get very upset when they know they are losing their home. Consequently, they "show off" on the way out and leave the individual in a streak of pain. Thankfully, this does not last long.

We once had a demon scream, "I hate her!" and in this case we believe the demon was telling the truth, although they are usually liars. You see, demons DO hate you and, in fact, they even hate each other. We once had a demon tell us that he would not come out until we called out another particular demon that it named. We were not even aware of the second demon and would not have addressed it. Obviously, the first demon knew that we were unaware of its presence and it made him jealous that he was getting kicked out and the other one wasn't.

After deliverance, the demons try very hard to get back into the house they were forced to leave. They always refer to the person we are praying for as their home.

After Keisha was delivered, she had a "slip" and was

overcome by temptation and yielded to sin. In this way she opened the door for the return of the demons, but she immediately called us and asked for an appointment. She didn't give them time to build a stronghold in her life. This is very important! Do you stay in the garbage dump of SIN or do you cry out to the living GOD? God wants to pick you up, brush you off, and set your feet back on solid ground. Keisha did the right thing!

DON'T PREJUDGE!—CLAIRE

This following account tells of a deliverance that I thought would not take much time, but, boy, was I wrong!

Donna was an accomplished, sharp businesswoman who appeared to have her act together. She was on fire for God, and was a strong witness for Jesus Christ in her workplace. During our first two visits, we realized that she was living above some very adverse circumstances in her background.

I had gotten our appointment times mixed up, so Paul and I were taking our time eating breakfast and getting dressed. In fact, I had just mentioned to Paul that our first appointment would be real easy and wouldn't take long. And right then the phone rang! The church was calling to let us know our appointment was waiting for us. Our day instantly turned to chaos. It seemed that everything went wrong that could go wrong. On our drive to the church, I told Paul that evidently there was going to be a mighty deliverance with someone that day.

When we met with Donna, she told us that everything imaginable had happened to her that morning to keep her from coming for deliverance. After sharing our experiences of opposition, we all realized just how important this session was going to be.

We were absolutely right! Demons began talking through Donna and the spirit of infirmity that had taken the form of diabetes told us that it would not come out because it had been in the family for thousands of years. Well, it DID come out, but it was very angry about leaving. The spirit taunted, "I'll just go into her daughter when I leave." We expect this, so we always apply the holy and precious blood of Jesus Christ to the individual's entire family before we begin the deliverance.

When Paul called out a spirit of depression, the demon said, "I am on assignment! I have been appointed to kill her!" Four spirits screamed out that they were going to kill her: depression, infirmity, heaviness, and suicide. A spirit of loneliness begged Paul, "Please don't make me leave! I don't have anyplace to go!"

The demons in Donna growled like dogs and said they were going to come back. But Donna was delivered completely that day! After deliverance, the demons can't come back unless you invite them in.

HIGH PRIESTESS—CLAIRE

The first time I saw Sabrina, she was lying on the floor of the platform of our church and the pastor's wife was praying for her. The pastor's wife asked me to set up an appointment for Sabrina to see us about deliverance counseling. When Sabrina and I spoke by telephone the next day to set a date, she told me she had been a high priestess in the Satanic Movement. Even though we did set a date and time, Sabrina did not show up for her appointment, so we called her and she indicated that she had changed her mind about counseling.

About seven months later, I found a note in my church mailbox from Sabrina stating that she felt if she didn't get deliverance, she would surely die! In the note she told me her occult name and the names of twenty-five demons that had been assigned to her since birth.

Sabrina's first appointment was very profitable and we felt she had a sincere desire to be delivered. She was very open and shared a lot with us. She had been programmed as a small child to be a participant in the Satanic Movement. She said that during the month-long programming, the movement tortured her so badly that in order to cope, she would take on personalities other than her own.

Sabrina learned that members of the Satanic Movement went to great expense to make sure someone was around her at all times to spy on her. Your life is not really your own when you are involved in the occult. She had a very good friend when she was growing up who lived directly across the street and she later found out that this little boy's family had been located there specifically to spy on her.

According to Sabrina, the movement was seriously upset with her because they knew she was leaving. They had been leaving dead animal parts on her front porch and she had even found a dead buzzard hanging in a tree in her front yard. One morning she called us in a distraught state because the picture of her little boy was missing from her key chain. She knew the key chain was in her purse when she went to bed but the picture was missing out of it the next morning. She had double dead bolt locks on her doors and there was no way anyone could have entered the house! But someone or something had taken that picture.

Sabrina lived in such terror that the night before Halloween, she came to church just to be comforted by the presence of the Lord.

Sabrina had told us that her phones were tapped and I knew this was true because we could hear evidence of it on a message she had left on our answering machine. We heard two separate people hanging up the phone. She lived in a world of suspicion and distrust, yet she was made privy to extremely sensitive information. She told us that the reason she could not finish her homework for the deliverance session was because she had found out some very confidential information that had upset her.

When it was time for Sabrina's deliverance, she came to the appointment but was unprepared because her homework was not done. It was a little puzzling to us, because she drove quite a long time from another town and it really was inconvenient.

Sabrina came back another day and she had done her homework, so she was ready. Deliverance day for Sabrina took us to a new level of ministry! We always break ungodly soul ties before we begin to pray deliverance, and Sabrina named eighteen people (not including her parents) with whom she had ungodly soul ties. She had blood covenants with some of them and others were people who had programmed her. She repeatedly called out the name Damien but she did not know why; she said she did not even know anyone named Damien. When we broke the soul tie between her and Damien, that spirit manifested more mightily than all the others.

We called out multi-personalities, and even though there was a big manifestation, nothing was leaving. Then we called out a personality of high priestess and it screamed on its way out. We started to call out another personality, but the Holy Spirit interrupted us and let us know that we needed to break the ungodly soul tie between Sabrina and satan before we continued. We began to break this soul tie and found ourselves wrestling with a power that called himself satan. This was awesome, but we felt no fear at all! The devil spoke forth in a very hateful voice, "**I would be God if it weren't for His b_____d Son!**" (The word he used meant that the mother did not have a husband.)

Sabrina was getting full deliverance from everything that we were calling forth because she was ready! One of her homework assignments had been to make a list of the people she needed to forgive, a list of all occult involvement, and all sexual activities outside marriage. As we always do, we had Sabrina burn this list of names, and when she burned the paper, she told us that voices actually screamed out.

Demon Slayers

We make it a practice to pray over each other and the room before we see anyone. We dispatch mighty warring angels to be stationed around the room, then move around the room to cover it with anointing oil. We pray over the oil that it will be a symbol of the blood of Jesus Christ and the Holy Spirit. Since this room was so anointed, everything was going along nicely as long as we stayed there. But after ministering for about three hours, I needed to go to the ladies' room and Sabrina decided to go with me.

Sabrina left the ladies' room and I assumed she had returned to the prayer room. However, she and Paul were nowhere in sight and I finally spotted them outside in the parking lot. Sabrina was sitting in her van and Paul was standing outside the van talking to her. She had slipped out to go home and Paul was trying to persuade her to go back inside. "Sabrina, come back in. We are not finished!" She replied in a voice that was definitely not Sabrina's, "Sabrina is not here and she can't hear a word you're saying." The voice was manly and spoke with a thick New York accent.

When I approached the van, Sabrina was pulling out a cigarette and offered me a smoke. She began combing her hair in a different style and remarked, "I feel like a greased pig! Thanks for the new hairdo." I always use anointing oil in my hands when we pray for people as it helps with the deliverance. Since we pray that the oil is the symbol of the blood of Jesus, the devils cannot stand it. They hate the blood of Jesus!

Sabrina turned on the car radio and started to swing with the music. I couldn't quite understand what she was muttering, but it seemed like she was taking credit for writing the song. Somehow we got her out of the van, but she was not Sabrina—she was a totally different person. The transformation was startling! She was like a man, rough, crude, rude, like a criminal you would not like to meet in a dark alley. This personality strutted around with shoulders squared and pushed back, legs spread apart while walking,

66

hands on her hips, cigarette hanging from her mouth. The New York accent was pronounced and the words she spoke were foul and blasphemous. She walked like she owned the world and was afraid of nothing. Her face became fixed like stone, hard and unflinching, and her eyes became like a wild animal, darting back and forth.

She kept strutting and looking back and forth, like she was expecting someone to pass by. She said to Paul, "You see that bird up there? It's a seagull and I hate seagulls! I kill them. Do you wanna watch me kill it?" Then she started bragging about how many people she had killed. Without warning she smiled at me with a crazed look and said, "I'm going to cut you!"

After she threatened me, she looked at her watch and said, "I gotta go. I've got a $20,000 deal going down across town." At that moment I said to her, "Sabrina, let's go inside. I'm getting cold out here in the rain." She replied with a taunting voice, "You're just a wimp! I've just come from New York and I was walking barefoot in snow three feet deep. There ain't no weather gonna bother me." All the time she spoke, she kept her head high and looked down her nose at us.

"Maybe I can appeal to her motherhood," I thought, since she had a young son. "Sabrina, I don't think your son would appreciate a person like you for a mother." Then this personality replied, "#$%*#$%* ... I taught him how to smoke. I can take care of him a whole lot better than Sabrina can (then more cursing). I've given him all the expensive games any kid could want."

I kept asking her to tell us her name but she just smiled back at us with that goofy smile. "Do you think I'm stupid? Youse guys ain't seen a real spirit yet! All youse have been messin' with is the small stuff. Now youse are gonna see what a real spirit is and I ain't gonna leave." Then I would call for Sabrina and this personality would say, "Sabrina can't even hear you!"

We challenged her with, "If you're so brave, why won't you come back into the church building?" She pulled herself real straight, looked at the church, and replied, "I ain't never been in a church before!" I told her I didn't think she was so brave if she was afraid to come in and sit down in a children's nursery (where we were meeting that day). That seemed to get to her, because she agreed to come back in. I walked on ahead to enter the building but when I looked behind me, she and Paul weren't following. They were still outside. She turned and started for her van, but Paul was right behind her and stopped her. "Oh, I see you're smarter than the other one," she said to him.

During this entire time, we had a powerful prayer team supporting us inside the church. When I went back outside, she jumped out of the van and said, "The last people that tried to deliver Sabrina got left mighty bloody. Do youse want the same?" Paul replied, "Let's go inside and see what happens." After his comment, she seemed eager to go back inside—I think she got energized at the prospect of destroying the place and cutting us up.

Back in the room, Paul and I sat down but Sabrina remained standing. She walked directly over to the room's air conditioning unit, which was about five feet off the floor, and, to my absolute surprise, found a pair of very large, pointed scissors lying there. She grabbed those scissors and unexpectedly assumed a stabbing position, walking rapidly toward Paul. Paul had his back to her at this point and didn't even realize she had found scissors, so I kicked him in the leg so he would turn around. When he saw her, he was as cool as a cucumber because even though he realized she meant to do him bodily harm, she would not be able to hurt him! I can truthfully say that I wasn't quite so sure! I thought, "Oh, dear, this deliverance is going to get bloody and probably end up in the newspaper. That won't look good for our church."

Pastor Benny Hinn had prophesied over Paul that he would

know God like Abraham did. Abraham was a man of great faith and that day I saw part of this prophecy come true right before my eyes. Paul was not afraid for one moment during this entire episode.

This personality paced back and forth and around us, all the while playing with the scissors, running her forefinger and thumb along the sharp edge while verbally threatening us. Her eyes had a strange expression in them and she acted like an insane person. Paul asked her why she had let Sabrina come for deliverance and she replied, "Oh, it was all part of the plan!"

As she continued to prance around the room, she said, "I was in Charles Manson, I was in Son of Sam, and I was the one who struck Jesus! Oh, yes, I was at Calvary! Oh, how I manipulated those people." She had a demented grin and her eyes darted back and forth while she ranted, "Oh, how I manipulated those people!" All the while she was telling us she was going to kill us, too.

This personality sat down in the chair and began to do incantations against us. She made many strange gestures with her hands and began speaking in an ungodly tongue and stomping her feet loudly. She made the motions of throwing objects at us, especially me, then found some paper, tore off a section, and cut out what resembled a face mask. The "mask" had two circles, a triangle, and four square boxes. She held the mask up to Paul and then to me. When she did her incantations, Paul and I raised our hands toward heaven and praised the Lord God of the universe. This made her extremely nervous and uneasy. Finally she asked, "What is this? Ain't youse guys gonna talk to me anymore?"

She got up from her chair and strutted around the room some more. She went over to a large extension cord plugged into the wall. The nursery room we were meeting in had no windows, so without artificial light, it is absolutely dark. You can't see a thing in that room, absolutely nothing, if the lights are out. I knew that she was going for the light switch and I knew that I did not want to be in a totally dark room with a demon. Especially when that demon had a pair of scissors in its hands! It occurred to me, also, that possibly she would put that mask on before she killed.

I got up and walked right past her, telling her, "If you are going to turn off the lights, I'm leaving." I was actually thinking, "If I'm going to get killed, I'm going to get killed in the light, not the dark. I am definitely not staying in this room with that demon." When I walked out of the room, I noticed a chair in the hall and I used it to prop open the door; then I left. She did flip the lights out, but Paul was not in complete darkness because the door was partially open and light from the hallway entered the room.

I was only gone for a short time and when I walked back into the room, Paul had the scissors in his hand and they were both seated. Sabrina still had the character of the other person but quite suddenly she jerked her head quickly, and she was Sabrina again!

Sabrina was not aware of anything that had happened during the previous forty minutes other than walking to the bathroom. Now she was back! She told us that someone had once told her that she had gone into a church carrying a very long knife and had tried to kill the pastor. She said the only thing she knew about that incident was what she had been told.

Later when Paul and I were discussing what had happened, I mentioned that he never seemed afraid. He replied, "Didn't you notice that she never got close to us? Those mighty warring angels that we dispatched all over the room were around us and she could not get close to us!"

When Sabrina came back to herself she was so sincere! She said, "I feel so much better!" She told us that during the deliverance she could see the devils leave. She was so filled with relief and joy that she began to laugh with a holy laughter. Many people laugh like this when they get fully delivered.

Sabrina gave us a list of demon names that had been assigned to her and we bound them up one by one. When we came to one named "Molech" (demon of murder), the demon manifested just like the person that she had become during that forty minutes of wild behavior. Now we knew the demon by name! I heard Paul say, "I bind you up, Molech, and I don't need any scissors to do it!"

The session that day took so long that Sabrina had to leave to pick up her son before we were completely finished with the deliverance. We bound up all the remaining devils in her so they could not bother her until she got back to us. Even though we had spent three hours with her, we barely scratched the surface of what she needed.

I asked a girl who was a former satanist what the symbols on the paper mask meant and she said the triangle meant "satan or satanism," the circles signified that "a war had been launched" and the squares meant "death." I took the paper mask home after the session. We covered it with anointing oil and burned it in the sink, reversing the curse back to the demon that sent it and commanding him to go out to the uninhabited places!

Sabrina later told us that she and several of her group had put some curses on a Christian. Nothing happened to the blood-bought Christian, but two of her group died and three got extremely ill. This was a clear display of the greater power of Jesus Christ and convinced her that she was on the wrong side. She knew she had to become a Christian after she witnessed this.

Ye are of God, little children, and have overcome them: because greater is he that is in you, than he that is in the world. (I John 4:4)

71

SPIRITS OF INSANITY—CLAIRE

Linda had a strange reaction when we commanded spirits of insanity and mind binding to leave her. She jerked back in the chair, tilting it backwards, and her eyes crossed. Frankly, it was really a stupid look.

As we got to know Linda better, she told us some very strange stories. She had been brought up on military property because her father was a high ranking military official. One of her memories involved playing with her little friends in a large dirt hole like many children do, but suddenly they found themselves in some sort of space ship. She then realized that she was lying on a table being examined by someone and she could see a friend on another table. This lasted only a little while, then they were all back in the ditch. They ran home and told their parents what had happened. A military officer came to the house and demanded to hear the entire story, then admonished her not to tell anyone what had happened. He said that what they had seen was a top military secret.

Another time Linda was given two smooth stones by an old lady she saw near a cave where she lived. She said the woman told her that there would come a time for her to give the stones to someone else and she would know when the time came. Linda had kept these two stones with her for years, through three failed marriages and now during her separation from her present husband.

At the time Linda came to see us, she was living in a center for abused women, but she had put a down payment down on an apartment and was ready to leave the women's center. As she was preparing to see us for a second appointment, she had an overwhelming urge to give those two stones to a woman living at the women's center with her. She found the stones in an old box where she had stored them, and took them to the lady at the center. As they talked, she found out that the woman had rented a room at the exact place where she, Linda, had rented a room. This so distressed Linda that she decided not to move there, even if she lost her deposit.

Linda had another strange story about the letters 968. She said that every day of her life, she thought about these numbers over and over. She could recall being in the woods at night with a lot of men and chickens everywhere. The day she came to see us, somebody scratched her car and she sketched us a picture of what the scratches looked like. Paul saw that the sketches resembled the letters 968 and figured that must have been some kind of trigger point that a satanist had used to control her.

Trusting our discernment on this, we commanded any demonic power that had entered her through the stones or through the numbers 968 to leave her, and her entire body began to shake uncontrollably. Then she screamed at the top of her lungs and ended up on the floor in a heap. But these things began to leave her in a hurry by the power of Jesus' Name!

Each demon that left Linda caused her tremendous pain in different parts of her body. She was absolutely exhausted when she left our office, but she looked great! We left a short time before she did and we saw her come out of the building. We both exclaimed, "Is that the same girl we just prayed for? She looks absolutely terrific—totally different!" It was remarkable.

Dear reader, it is important to note that Linda had been into New Age practices for a few years during her adult life and obviously had been into something occult as a child. If you are involved in anything that messes with your mind, such as meditation or hypnotism, you should RUN, NOT WALK away from it. No matter how innocent it may seem to you, it is a powerful tool of the devil to gain control of your mind. These types of things are definite entry points for a demon to take control!

We are in such a rewarding ministry, because we see results every time we pray deliverance for someone.

MOLESTED IN DIAPERS

We always break ungodly soul ties before we pray for a person's deliverance. Marilyn was a beautiful woman in her early thirties, a very gifted actress who had played a major role in a television series for ten years. She had played numerous roles in other productions over the years, and multi-personality spirits had attached themselves to her. We found that the multi-personality spirits would *not* leave until we broke the ungodly soul ties between her and the names of the characters that she had played.

When we began the deliverance, she mentioned that she had always had an uneasy feeling about her boy cousins, so we immediately broke anything that could be ungodly between them. She went on to tell us that when these cousins came to her house, she always went into her bedroom and stayed until they left. During the deliverance session, she screamed so loudly and so intensely that her face became blotchy and she screamed out, "It's my first birthday! I am still in my diapers! My cousins are holding me down—I can feel their hands on my wrists! They are sexually molesting me!"

She became so *intense* that *black patches* appeared under her eyes and she looked like she had been in a fight. We stopped her and had her do a proclamation "to choose to forgive her boy cousins." After that, we commanded those spirits to leave and they obeyed *immediately*.

Even though she had no memory of the incident until the time of deliverance, she had put a shield around herself and never let a relationship with a man come into her life. She was extremely beautiful, but she had never had a boyfriend. After we prayed, she accepted a date with a man that same week, and she told us later that she really enjoyed his company. "I told him that if he had asked me out a week earlier, I would not have accepted," she said. Now she is free to live a normal life and relate to the opposite sex without fear.

JESUS APPEARED

Bobby Jo was a plain woman in her mid-thirties who wore her drab, dark blond hair in a crew cut. Her rough mannerisms made her appear manly and we found out that she had been involved in lesbianism for many years. She had also been dabbling in the occult world since she was a teenager.

Bobby Jo had been born again for nine months when she came to see us. She had a deep hunger for the things of God and was devouring the Bible. She had made a complete turnaround in her life and was growing at an accelerated pace. She knew she had a call of God on her life and she was so eager to be on her way! However, she was wise enough to know that she had areas of bondage. That knowledge brought her to see us.

When we had our deliverance session with Bobby Jo, the demons threw her all over the room. The chair she was sitting in broke into two parts and she landed completely across the room. The deliverance was physically taxing and about half way through she just sat back, trying to catch her breath from the last encounter.

Bobby Jo was sitting quietly with her eyes closed, when without warning her arm shot out, she pointed to the corner of the room, and exclaimed, "Jesus is in this room! He is right over there!" She slowly rose from her chair and walked in the direction she had indicated. She really looked as if there was an invisible force field in front of her and she was pushing her way through it. As she proceeded, her body began to tremble violently and she almost fell backwards, but Paul caught her. Then she steadied herself and stood quietly with her arms wrapped around herself. She stood in that position for about fifteen minutes, not uttering a sound.

The atmosphere in the room was so holy that you hardly dared to breathe for fear of interrupting what the Spirit of God was doing. Then she spoke, "He's leaving. He's going up in the clouds back to heaven!"

What a holy time that was! We had to help Bobby Jo back into her chair, where she just sat with her hands toward heaven, praising God! Later, she told us that He had beckoned her to come over to Him in the corner of the room and when she obeyed, He held her in His arms. "He told me I was free!" The Lord told her many other things, too, but they were too private for her to share with us.

WATER DEATH CURSE—CLAIRE

Esther, a loving, concerned grandmother, came to us with an alarming story regarding her granddaughter. She related that approximately two years earlier, her granddaughter had fallen into a lake and nearly drowned. Paramedics were able to revive her and she had been in a comatose state ever since. Esther had legal custody of the child and asked if we would pray for her.

We went to the hospital and saw a fragile, delicate little girl lying in a coma, still and silent, unable to speak or move in any way. Her tiny arms, hands, legs and feet were twisted, an obvious symptom of her condition, but she was also blind, a not-so-obvious symptom. Our hearts were stricken as we looked at her and we knew it was time to proceed.

The first step in deliverance is counseling and we counsel with the parents or the person who is responsible for a child under the age of accountability. In this case, we counseled with Esther and discovered that both her mother and sister had drowned in separate accidents. It was evident to us that drowning was a water death curse on this family.

During the deliverance prayer session, we prayed for the granddaughter (with her grandmother sitting in proxy for her). There were no manifestations whatsoever as we prayed for Esther. But when we laid hands on Esther and prayed for *her granddaughter*, commanding the spirits to leave the child (through the grandmother), the spirits got violent. Esther began to look and act like a mad dog! She actually showed her teeth and started biting at the air.

When we called out a spirit of death and a curse of infirmity, the demons shook Esther like a rag whipping in the wind! They put up a tremendous resistance to leaving. We called out every single one by the medical name of the child's infirmities, and each one reacted when its name was called. Esther was exhausted by the time we finished, but her granddaughter was set free from the spirits of infirmity through the love and faith of her concerned grandmother. Esther called us a week later and told us that the child began improving the day we prayed. She was communicating with them within a week.

Not all infirmities and sicknesses are demonic, but this one definitely was!

FRIEND IN FLAMES—CLAIRE

Carrie had been waiting patiently for almost two years to get an appointment with us. When we were finally able to see her, she was so excited about the deliverance that she could hardly wait to do the homework we had given her! She had even fasted prior to the appointment.

As we gathered information about ungodly soul ties, right in the middle of it, the Lord told me, "FIRE!" The Lord spoke this word to me three times before I finally asked her, "Carrie, what about a fire?" Carrie was speechless for a moment, startled!

It seems that when she was about five years old, her little friend from next door had caught fire, right in front of her. Carrie had watched her friend burn. Later, in a tragic accident, Carrie was lighting a fire in a fireplace and the house suddenly ignited. The house burned quickly and there was nothing left but ashes.

The ungodly soul tie that needed to be broken was between her and her friend who had died. This had given an entry point for a spirit of fear to come into her life.

Although Carrie was born again and Spirit-filled, she could not live victoriously and be all that God wanted her to be because this fear was always holding her back. For her, life was like hitting a brick wall head-on. You cannot have perfect faith if you are plagued with a spirit of fear. Now that the spirit of fear is gone, she is experiencing perfect faith.

There is no fear in love; but perfect love casteth out fear: because fear hath torment. He that feareth is not made perfect in love. (I John 4:18)

Carrie is no longer a prisoner of fear, but is now experiencing perfect faith. She was also set free from a tremendous spirit of poverty. Since then, she has a new job and has received a settlement of an extremely large sum of money, all of which shows evidence of prosperity. Perfect faith and prosperity: what a victory!

Over the years, the Lord has given us insight on many of these ungodly soul ties that need to be broken.

FOUR ANGELS—CLAIRE

From looking at Lee, a beautiful, sweet Oriental woman in her mid-forties, one would never imagine that she had been extremely active in the occult world for most of her life!

We know that when someone has been very active in occult things, their "spiritual eyes" are opened in that world. We have noticed that when such a person turns to Christianity, they can still see into the demonic spirit world, only now they can also see God's angels. This happened right in our office while we were praying deliverance for Lee.

At one point during the prayer, she looked at Paul and started to laugh, "You have a huge crown on your head and it is full of big diamonds. But it doesn't fit on your head, it hovers an inch above your head. It is wider than your shoulders and the crown moves as you move."

Lee then turned toward me and put her hands up to her face. "Oh, you have one, too! But your crown is smaller than Paul's." She lowered her voice and whispered, "There are angels in this room. There are four of them, one in each corner, and they have different colored sashes around their waists. There's yellow, red, blue and green. The Lord is telling me that each color has great significance."

About a week later Lee called us so excited that she said she felt like she was about to jump out of her skin. She had been fasting and asking God this question: "How does the devil *know* the potential in a human life?" (It seems that the devil works harder to hold down and hinder those who have the greatest calling of God on their lives.) The Lord answered Lee by telling her that satan and his kingdom *know* potential because of the color of the sashes of the angels that are assigned to you at birth.

Lee shared the following insights that the Lord had revealed to her: "The diamonds in the crowns are souls you have helped set free; you are storing your riches in heaven. The crowns are God's protection and His covering on your lives."

She went on to explain the angels and the sashes: "The Lord showed me that the four angels I saw in the four corners of the room that day were your angels. Two of them belonged to Paul and two of them belonged to Claire. When you became one in marriage, you could then move in each other's gifts. The two angels assigned to Paul are yellow and green. The two angels assigned to Claire are red and blue." The colors of the sashes signified the following:

YELLOW	Truth, faith, call of a pastor
GREEN	Humility, leadership, deliverance, call of an apostle
RED	Wisdom, understanding, knowledge, call of a teacher
BLUE	Healing, joy of the Lord, call of a prophet

Lee told us that in answer to her specific prayer, the Lord told her that the devil recognizes potential because he knows the meaning of the colors of the sashes. In the spirit realm, devils and angels can see each other, and since the angels' sashes have special meanings, the demonic kingdom knows where to direct their greatest attack. Those with the greatest potential get hit with the greatest attack.

Some of the things we see and hear in this ministry are stunning. Absolutely amazing! There is never a dull day!

FACES OF EVE—CLAIRE

We had never before experienced as many different faces in one human being as Eve possessed. She was plagued with multi-personalities and when each one surfaced, it became totally believable and real. Each personality had its own distinctive facial expression and body language and as each new personality surfaced, it was difficult for us to believe that this was the same girl who had come to us begging for an appointment.

Eve's husband was in prison for sexually abusing their son, Ronnie. Ronnie had been removed from his mother's care and this left her in a serious suicidal state. She longed to be free! Her true "born-again" personality desperately wanted freedom and longed for deliverance. The other personalities were clearly terrified, but this did not stop the evil personalities from doing physical battle to keep their territory.

This deliverance session was very interesting and quite long. The personality that made Eve sad and depressed distorted her facial features and she looked like she was being tortured horribly. We encountered a personality of vanity and pride that would stand up and actually mock us and laugh, sneering as she looked down her nose at us.

When we discerned a personality of lust, perversion and whoredom and called out these spirits, they began to act extremely sensuous. That personality caused Eve to lick her lips slowly and make very seductive body movements. Her hair fell across her face and her eyes begged Paul for his attention. The demon obviously was trying to beguile him, perhaps because it thought it could persuade Paul not to command it to go. But he rose up mightily, and with all power and authority in the Name of Jesus, he commanded the multi-personality spirit to leave. He called the spirit "Cassandra" because Eve told us that someone named Cassandra would take over her body at night, causing her to do evil things she ordinarily would never do.

We really had a battle with these multi-personalities, but the victory was oh, so sweet! Eve doesn't have to fight them anymore. She no longer cries for freedom, because Jesus made her free forever—and she is a wonderful, beautiful person that people love to be around.

THE COCAINE ADDICT—CLAIRE

We have counseled numerous cocaine addicts because once one gets delivered, he spreads the word to all his friends and then we have a waiting list.

John had been in prison for drug-related reasons and when this huge, rugged man came to us, he was mean, rude, intimidating and seemed like he wanted to fight. Paul discerned a spirit of jealousy and when he commanded it to leave, John manifested with so much anger that it seemed he wanted to kill Paul.

We called out spirits of hatred, rage, and murder and the spirits completely took over the man. The demon spoke right through John. "You don't know who I have killed!" His eyes gleamed with hatred, his face contorted, and he screamed, "You don't know his name!"

Paul stared right back and firmly said, "It doesn't matter who you have killed. It is all under the blood of Jesus, anyway. Jesus died so that John is forgiven, and when Jesus forgives, He forgets it and then it is as if it never happened! John is *not guilty* but you *are guilty! Now come out of him in the Name of Jesus*! This is not your house anymore."

John rose out of his chair and with a very LOUD AND LONG SCREAM, that demon was history. What a struggle! But what a victory!

TOTAL MEMORY LOSS—CLAIRE

Paul and I were looking forward to having some free time that Saturday because we had had two individuals cancel their deliverance sessions. However, early that morning, a couple from another state called, urging us to make time for them because they had to return home that evening.

Mary and her husband had listened to all our tape teachings and had done all the homework assignments. So, even though we were tired and thought the Lord had arranged some free time for us, we felt a real urgency to see them.

Mary confided to us that she had suffered many problems connected to the mind and had been to a psychiatrist. One of the major dilemmas she had was that she had absolutely no memory of her youth. As we talked about the mental problems that tormented her constantly, I discerned that her father had sexually abused her. When I asked her about this, she reacted strongly and almost snapped at me, "I just can't go there!" What she meant was that she didn't want to tap into her memories to find out more about this.

Paul commanded mind binding spirits to leave and her head started to shake uncontrollably. Her hands flew to her head and she held it as if she thought it was going to explode! But when those spirit left, it was very dramatic

Paul commanded a spirit of forgetfulness to leave in Jesus' Name. As that spirit left, Paul commanded that *memory* come in, and *instantly* Mary bent over and began to sob like her heart would literally break! She cried for almost half an hour and between sobs, she told us that all the memories had come back.

As Mary poured out her sorrow and pain, I spoke softly to her, telling her to *choose* to forgive, no matter how bad the memory was. She kept nodding her head, as if to say, "Yes, yes, yes! I forgive!" And she truly *did* forgive, because all of a sudden the crying stopped and the laughter started. She laughed with the joy of victory, knowing that finally it was over, once and for all!

Mary discovered what the devil had hoped to keep covered up in her memory lapse. He wanted to keep her in bondage to the trauma, but the Holy Spirit uncovered it and set her free. She made the correct choice in forgiving and she was GLORIOUSLY SET FREE!

All the tears Mary shed were healing tears, and when it was over, it was over for good. That's the way it is with deliverance. The memory may still be there, but it has no power! The sting of the memory is gone.

BLINDED BY DEMONS—CLAIRE

We need to preface this account by confessing that sometimes we are quite taken aback by what the demonic kingdom can do to a person in the physical realm.

We were praying deliverance for a young man, Sam, who had practiced homosexuality for as long as he could remember. Sam was short and frail, and his speech and gestures were very feminine. As in the case of most, he had been sexually abused as a very young boy. As we continued in his deliverance, we witnessed something quite out of the ordinary. While we were praying for him, Sam suddenly became blind! As strange as it may seem, not only could he not see, but his eyes were "milky" from a white film which covered them.

Then, to top things off, he began slipping in and out of a trance-like state and, frankly, this was quite frightening to me (Claire), because we were not able to bring him out of it. He was absolutely panic stricken. Every time he would snap out of his trance, he would go into hysterics, screaming at the top of his lungs, "I'M BLIND! I'M BLIND!"

After about twenty minutes, Sam calmed down and told us that he actually felt the demons leave him through his eyes. We then realized that the demons had gained their legal right to be there through the "lust of the eye." But they had lost that right and reluctantly made their exit. There is no doubt that the demons put Sam through a frightful experience (and caused us some anxiety, as well), but the outcome was GLORIOUS! Not only did Sam's eyesight return, but he was totally and completely set free.

Many times a demon spirit will leave a person through pain, but this was the first time we had ever seen a person go completely blind. People who have experienced pain during deliverance have told us that the pain only lasted for a few moments. Our guess is that the demons are so furious over losing custody of their home that they don't know what else to do except throw a temper tantrum on the way out. But I have to say that Sam is the first person we have ever seen go completely blind. That spirit *really* wanted to show off on its way out. We believe the demon was able to blind Sam because the lust of the eye had allowed it to come in in the first place, giving it the legal right to be there. Another example of why we have to be so careful about what we put before our eyes!

We command demons to leave a person in a particular order. Over the years we have discovered that three large STRONGHOLDS are dominant in homosexuals/lesbians: the spirits of lying, whoredom, and perversion. They seem to be intertwined like a rope and if you get rid of these three, the spirit of homosexuality and lesbianism will leave quickly. However, if you don't get rid of the stronghold spirits first, you can pray all day and those spirits will not leave. Bind the strong man and spoil his house.

No man can enter into a strong man's house, and spoil his goods, except he will first bind the strong man; and then he will spoil his house. (Mark 3:27)

NO DIVORCE NOW!

A counselor from a neighboring church referred a young couple to us because he believed they needed deliverance. The husband was very good-looking and had a high-paying marketing job. His wife was tall, slender, and beautiful, and she was also very sweet, kind and intelligent.

To look at this couple, one would assume they had everything going for them. But there was one big problem in their marriage: he could not break his crack cocaine habit! She was completely worn down from dealing with his problem and the side effects on their marriage. Even though he was very successful financially, he spent all his income to feed his habit. He had even sold everything of value that they owned in order to get money for cocaine. It was a desperate situation.

This young man obviously was ready for deliverance, because he was set free very quickly that day. We have noticed that many people try to cope with their problems, but it is so much better to just get *rid of them* once and for all!

You can take whatever spirit of bondage has you bound and

cope with it, but that never works forever. For instance, someone wants to quit smoking, so they replace that appetite with food, eating to excess and gaining a lot of weight. The same spirit of bondage is at work but it now has a different face and a new set of rules and demands. Instead of being in bondage to nicotine, the person is now in bondage to food. If you get delivered, you are set TOTALLY FREE of all bondage and addictions—forever!

YELLOW HANDS

Recently a well-known woman named Vivian came to us for deliverance. After several weeks of counseling, instruction, and preparation, we felt it was time to proceed with her deliverance.

During the deliverance session, we discerned that there was an ungodly soul tie between her and a girlfriend who had committed suicide three years earlier. While we were in the process of breaking this ungodly soul tie, the demon in her began screaming, twisting, and thrashing her body about. It was obvious that this demon was furious and wanted to fight. We were thankful that the battle was short and the ungodly soul tie was broken. Afterwards, we commanded a spirit of suicide to leave her, as well, and again, this spirit created a tremendous commotion and resistance before leaving.

Next, we called out a spirit of death, and as soon as we called it forth, we witnessed something we had never seen before. Vivian's hands instantly changed colors, turning yellow, beginning at her fingertips and going up to her elbows. It looked like she suddenly had developed jaundice.

After the deliverance session, we mentioned her hands to her, because we had all noticed the manifestation. She told us this had happened to her before, when her husband was dying. While he lay dying, he had grasped her hands tightly and would not let go. As soon as her husband expired, Vivian looked at her hands and noticed that they had become yellow. We knew right away that a spirit of death had transferred to her when her husband died.

The yellow appearance changed back to normal immediately after we came against that spirit of death and cast it out. When the color changed back to normal, it started at her elbows and went right out her fingertips—the reverse of how it entered. And it left much faster than it had come. Whoosh! It was gone!

NOTE:
There was an ungodly soul tie between Vivian and her friend, and also her husband, that allowed the spirit of death to enter.

VOODOO—CLAIRE

Sammy had lived in a third world country as a child and had moved to the Tampa Bay area as a teenager. In his native country he had observed his parents' activities in Santeria, an occult religion which combines West African and Roman Catholic beliefs. This opened many doors for occult activity in his life. After Sammy moved to Tampa, he accepted Jesus Christ as Lord and Savior, but he was in bondage to something that made him behave irrationally and violently.

Sammy was married to a wonderful young woman and they had three lovely children, but he often had a spirit of suspicion overcome him. He was so suspicious of his wife that he would call her almost every hour of the day to check on her. He accused her of having affairs and doing other things behind his back, even though she was a faithful, born-again Christian woman. This spirit of suspicion was totally controlling Sammy, even affecting his work and certainly affecting his home life.

Sammy's wife persuaded him to attend two counseling sessions, then we set a date of his deliverance prayer session. However, before that date came, he bolted into our office crying, "You have to pray for me now! I can't wait for my prayer date. Something is telling me to go home and kill my family, then myself." We instructed him to stay with his sister for the night, since we were not able to pray for him right at that moment.

The next morning Sammy came to our office for prayer. It was normally our day off, but we felt the urgency of the need and we were concerned for the welfare of his family.

During our prayer for Sammy, we called out a spirit of jealousy and suspicion, and immediately he began to manifest. My hands were on his shoulders and the spirit tried to bite my hands, so I put my hands on his back. Then the spirit in him tried to bite his own arms and shoulders. At that point Paul commanded the spirit, "Don't you hurt him, in Jesus' Name!" The spirit began to rip his shirt from one shoulder to the other, and when the session was over, there was shirt fabric all over the floor. He left our office with little shreds of shirt hanging from his shoulders. But he left with a smile on his face, beaming from ear to ear because he was finally set free!

Sammy was so thrilled to be free from the torment he had suffered for so long before his deliverance. We praise God every time we see His mercy and power set someone free.

Many times a demon in the husband knows exactly what to do or say to trigger a demon in the wife (and vice versa). Demons of anger, strife, argument and violence feed off each other. Whenever there is strife, those demons get fed their lunch; when they get hungry for dinner, they cause the couple to argue some more! You see, the couple's fighting just feeds the devils and empowers them to get bigger and stronger. QUIT ARGUING! Starve those demons! When you get rid of them through deliverance, the strife disappears and the marriage is healed.

THE EVIL NECKLACE THAT RETURNS

Tom answered the pastor's invitation to come forward for special prayer. When he got to the front, he fell to the floor, shaking uncontrollably. His face contorted and he stuck out his tongue in a strange way.

Tom was wearing a silver, rectangular necklace. Adorned with a sun, a star and a crescent moon, it was large and gaudy.

Someone close to him removed the necklace and laid it to the side. Inexplicably Tom calmed down, quit shaking, and looked normal. When he settled down, the person next to him picked up the necklace and started to put it in Tom's pocket for safekeeping. But when he got the necklace close to Tom, the "symptoms" started again, so the man pulled the necklace away—and Tom calmed down! The man "tested" the necklace several more times and got the same results!

We were asked to see Tom for counseling and deliverance and we found out that a former girlfriend (who was in the occult) had given the necklace to him. We immediately instructed him to get rid of the necklace because it obviously had a curse on it.

Tom told us later that he had taken the necklace home, thrown it in the trash can, and put the trash can on the curb for the next day's pick-up. However, the next day, after the trash had been picked up, the necklace appeared back on his bedroom dresser! He then disposed of the necklace in another manner and prayed over it, using the Name and blood of Jesus to make sure that it did not return a second time.

When we prayed deliverance, Tom was completely set free and he was so excited that he called his brother and told him he needed to have deliverance! It seems that all their ancestors had been steeped in the occult and Tom wanted to get all of them delivered. He now knew the truth!

Tom's brother came to us and begged us for an appointment, but we had a waiting list of three years at that time and it was difficult for us to work anyone else into our schedule. However, since Tom and his brother were roommates, we felt it was in their best interest to see the brother and we did, with good results! When people live together (husband, wife, children, roommates), we like to pray for all of them either on the same day or just as soon as possible.

DEMON ENTRY POINTS

Wanda, a striking, successful, professional woman, was frantic! When we first saw her, she wept so hard for the first half-hour that we sat just waiting until she could talk to us.

Wanda was very concerned about confidentiality, because she was from a socially prominent, renowned family. We assured her of complete privacy, which is our practice with *everyone* we see.

Wanda's husband had left her for another woman, who practiced witchcraft, and Wanda was devastated. She needed answers and did not know where to turn, so she went to a psychiatrist. He, in turn, referred her to a person who was into Santeria (the religion which mixes false gods with Catholic saints), and not knowing any better, she began attending their meetings. She got into their rituals and the man who was head of this particular group fell in love with her and wanted to make her a high priestess. She realized she had become involved in something way out of her control but she found that it was not easy to get out!

Whenever this group leader called her, she was compelled to go because they had cast a sort of spell over her. When she answered her phone to speak with any of this group, they would play a specific song and she would be under their power.

Miraculously, Wanda heard the salvation message and

accepted Jesus Christ as her personal savior. She knew she needed deliverance, so she came to us. During our first prayer session, we broke an ungodly soul tie between her and the leader of the occult group. When we did this, we felt an awesome force of what seemed like the whole demonic kingdom come against us!

We found out that during some of the rituals the group did over Wanda, they had cut her body in many places, causing an entry point for a demon at every cut. And, believe me, there was lots of demons! During Wanda's deliverance, the demons exited through those same cut places, causing her extreme, momentary pain.

Wanda is so free! She is one of the most godly, spiritual women you would ever hope to meet, and she is in church every time the doors are open. She flies all over the world attending Christian conferences where she can learn more about Him, and her hunger for the Word of God is more pronounced every time we see her. What a glorious deliverance she had!

WARRIOR SPIRIT—CLAIRE

Chung, a soft-spoken Korean man, had been a champion in martial arts since childhood; in fact, he came from a long line of champions. At the time he came to us, he was a black belt and a teacher of martial arts.

After his counseling sessions were completed, we told him we had set aside two hours for his deliverance session and he said quietly, "It will take much longer than that." Even though we were mildly surprised at that comment, we didn't attach too much importance to it. This man seemed very meek and shy, but later we found that he had told someone he had a "dark side." He warned his friend that if that side of him ever showed up, the friend should get as far away from him as possible—and as quickly as possible!

In his prayer session, we came to see what he was talking

about. As we do in all deliverance prayers, we commanded the part of his personality that was not "born again" to depart and nothing happened. We were aware that there were multi-personalities present but we knew from experience that until you discern them and can call them all by name, they will hide. It is extremely important to be specific concerning different personalities.

Chung sat in a chair, I stood behind him with my hands on his shoulders, and Paul sat across from Chung. Paul addressed the "warrior" personality—and it came forth like a LION. Chung began doing karate movements with his hands (even though Paul was holding onto his hands as tightly as he could), then he went straight for Paul's throat. As I watched this unfold, my faith level went down considerably and I began to get a little nervous. At other times when we have encountered an overpowering spirit getting out of control, I would summon a strong man to help us, but today no one was around.

When Chung went for Paul's throat, I began to call out Chung's name. Whenever a demon has taken over a person, calling out the name of the person usually gets them back to themselves. So I called Chung by name and Paul looked at me with wide eyes, "Don't do that! Let's get rid of this devil RIGHT NOW." Well, in my opinion "right now" wasn't looking too good and I wanted to have Paul around a long time. Negative thoughts bombarded my mind.

I was wrestling with Chung, too, trying to hold him in his chair. Finally, I sat down beside him because we have found that spirits of rage, murder, violence, hatred and anger want you to fight with them. They will struggle with you and if you struggle back, they LOVE IT. Your struggle feeds and empowers them. However, if you take your hands off the person, that spirit will usually stop manifesting—and that is exactly what happened.

I tried to talk to Chung and discovered that I was speaking to the devil that had taken control of him. Since the spirit knew that he was not going to get anywhere with Paul because Paul never once felt fear or doubt, he decided to direct his attention to me. The spirit tried to intimidate me and told me that it would kill me; then he asked me if I would like him to show me *how* he would kill me.

I was looking directly into Chung's eyes as I conversed with the spirit and to my utter surprise, the pupil in the middle of his eye (the little black circle) turned milky white and grew to about twice its normal size. I was so fascinated with that "white pupil" that I didn't look into the other eye to see if the same thing was happening. I had never seen anything like this before! I kept talking, but my mind was asking, "What in the world is going on here?"

Suddenly Chung's mouth turned into a sneer and he was staring at me with that strange eye! I kept calling Chung's name, hoping he would come back to himself. I verbally agreed with him that he could kill and that he could probably kill multiple persons. Then I warned him that if he killed someone, he would go to prison. A point of clarification here: a warrior spirit deludes a person into thinking that it (the spirit) will be his protection forever. But warrior spirits have spoken to us and told us that they do not like prison and will not go into prison with a person. The spirits simply go into someone else

I continued to try to reason with Chung, telling him that the warrior spirit wanted to kill him, that it hated him and one day would take him over if he did not get rid of it. I also warned Chung that he could end up hurting or killing someone he loved. I explained thoroughly (again) that God is the power that does the work of deliverance and he, Chung, must be willing to let it happen.

Paul and I are *nothing* but vessels to be used of God to speak forth His authority to make the demons leave a person. We again explained to Chung that if he wanted to hang on to this spirit, it would never leave him. I knew in my spirit that this demon was trying to convince Chung to let

93

it stay. And the demon was going back to its old argument that Chung needed it for protection. The same old lie.

I explained again to Chung that the warrior spirit was there for evil purposes (to kill, steal and destroy). I tried to convince him that the Spirit of God in him (Chung) had all power and authority to protect him. God is the ultimate protection over satan and his kingdom.

The battle was being waged in Chung. Again he snarled at Paul, growled loudly, and pointed toward a picture of the Lion of Judah hanging on our wall. The picture shows the pierced paws of the lion, and as Chung pointed, he said, "I was the one who drove the nails in Jesus' hands and I am going to drive them in your hands, too."

I reached for a bottle of anointing oil that was sitting on the desk. We had prayed over this oil and asked God to make it a symbol of the blood that Jesus had shed on Calvary. As soon as I poured some on Chung's head THE DEMON WENT CRAZY. Chung broke his hands free from Paul and grabbed his own head. When he got the oil on his hands, he began to shake them so violently that we were afraid he would hurt himself. It seemed like he would shake his hands completely off.

But here's the miracle! That warrior personality left through his hands and he almost collapsed, closing his eyes and bowing his head for quite some time. He stayed bowed in a posture of reverence to the Lord of Lords and King of Kings because the Lord had just proven Himself *all powerful over the forces of satan* and his kingdom. And Chung was right; it took more than two hours for him to be completely set free from all the evil baggage that he had picked up over the years.

Two weeks later we had the pleasure and joy of seeing Chung in a church service, kneeling before the Lord, tears streaming down his face, worshipping the God of all power and creation!

Interestingly, we have had two demon spirits speak to us and brag that they were responsible for driving the nails in Jesus and piercing His side. We believe that all satan's kingdom was there at the crucifixion and probably most of them resided in the Roman soldiers!

CATHOLIC MEN—CLAIRE

Once a month we hold a four-day seminar for anyone who wants to attend. During this seminar we conduct a group deliverance session with everyone present.

Recently, Paul took our car to be repaired and Ken, the shop owner, asked Paul what he did for a living. When Ken (a Catholic) found out we were in deliverance, he went wild with emotion. "I was just praying that the Lord would lead me to someone who knows and understands deliverance!" He attended a session and was so impressed by what he saw that he went back to his church and told everyone about the sessions. There was such a drastic change in his life that several men he knew realized they needed deliverance, as well.

Ken had purchased a large supply of our teaching materials and spent all his free time taking the men through the counseling teaching and the related homework. Then he called and asked if we would hold a deliverance session for them. He not only brought them to the session, but he even helped out in the deliverance itself.

Henry, one of the men Ken brought, began to manifest tremendously when Paul called out a familiar spirit from his inherited bloodline. Henry immediately stiffened up and his hands became twisted and deformed. Paul asked him if anyone in his family had arthritis or palsy and he answered that his mother was plagued with arthritis and his father had palsy. Those spirits had attached themselves to Henry and even though they were dormant, they were just waiting for the right time to manifest. The other two friends who had come with Ken were astonished at what they saw happening and as their friend continued to manifest demons, they almost lost it!

Paul commanded the familiar spirits to leave in Jesus' Name, and as he spoke, Henry's body and hands went from being totally rigid to completely limp as each spirit left. Then Paul came against the spirit of infirmity, and as the spirit fled, Henry's left ear opened up and he could hear. He had been completely deaf in that ear. He also received healing from constant pain in his elbow that had been plaguing him for ten years.

After the session, Henry picked up the chair and looked under it. When Paul asked if he had lost something, Henry replied, "I thought that you had wired the chair because it felt like 220 volts of electricity went through my body. I'm still numb from the waist down."

These men were set free by the power of God and it has certainly caused a stir in their church. Our phone is still ringing with others wanting to attend our seminars.

DEMON TORN FROM HIS SIDE—CLAIRE

Paul and I were strolling through a department store when Ben saw us and approached with such force we thought he was going to attack us! He was furious and didn't hesitate to let us know it.

"Don't you know I've got to get help? Don't you know I'm going to kill somebody if I don't get delivered? The other day I almost killed a guy because he cut me off in traffic! You promised me an appointment but I can't wait! I've got to see you!" He was talking and gesturing with such vehemence that I thought he was going to hit one of us— fury poured out of him. We managed to get him an appointment in a couple of weeks.

Ben was right on time for his appointment, but Paul and I had just been through the harrowing experience described earlier in which the high priestess in the Satanist Movement had tried to kill us with scissors. We were absolutely exhausted, both physically and emotionally, when Ben showed up. I dare say we were in a state of semi-shock from the struggle of the previous few hours.

Ben was a healthy young body builder who had been abused as a child and had lived for many years on the streets. He had been in a lot of trouble and was tormented by many spirits, including anger, hate, revenge and retaliation. He had tried to commit suicide at one time and was placed in a mental institution.

We started the session by breaking the ungodly soul ties between him and his father, and with the speed of lightning the demon reacted. As I usually do during prayer, I was standing behind Ben's chair. Absolutely without warning, he bolted out of the chair with such speed and force that I was thrown into the air and smashed against the wall about six feet behind me. I crumpled onto the floor for a moment, then gathered my wits about me, got up, and said to Paul, "We need some help in here."

"No, no, everything will be okay. We don't need anyone else to help." Both Paul and Ben assured me that all was well.

"That's easy for you to say," I thought. "You're not the one that just got knocked against the wall and landed on the floor."

I went along with the deliverance for a few more minutes until Ben again jumped up with the strength of a herd of horses. He would move so suddenly that there was no way to avoid him if he came toward you. I went out into the hall and found one of the strongest men on the church staff, a "muscle man" who resembled a bouncer. He didn't hesitate to go in the room with me, probably because he could see the desperation in my eyes and hear it in my voice.

We continued to pray for Ben and whenever we called out the spirits of anger, hatred, revenge and retaliation, he reacted so fiercely that it took all three of us to hold him. When Paul called out the spirit of revenge, Ben tore out of our grip with the speed of light, raised up off the floor, did a flip in mid-air, and landed on the floor, face down. We have never before or since seen such a strong demonic force! But when Ben got up off the floor, he was a different person. His watch and change were lying all over the floor because the pockets of his jeans were ripped from top to bottom. We were all so stunned we just stood there and stared at each other amazement. It was unbelievable—but it had really happened!

The following morning Ben called to ask if we could bring a camera with us to church that evening. We agreed, and asked him why. "You will have to see it to believe it. I really can't describe what I'm looking at." That evening we saw what Ben was talking about. When that last demon left him, it left him with a HUGE spot on his side that looked exactly like claw marks. A registered nurse in our church made the remark that the wound was obviously made from the inside out instead of the other way around.

All of us in the room during Ben's deliverance knew that no one had touched his side. Paul was holding his wrists, the staff member had hold of one wrist and a shoulder, and I had my hands on both his shoulders. When the demon left, it broke free and literally flew up into the air! Paul took a picture of Ben's side and we put it on our deliverance tape entitled "Deliverance From Satan's Torment."

What a day that had been. First the woman with the scissors, then Ben's difficult deliverance. We were really glad when that day was over! But most of all, we were glad that, once again, God had the victory over the devil in both deliverances. Praise God!

GABRIEL PEACE—CLAIRE

The man came to all of his counseling appointments and didn't speak with anyone. He politely greeted us, but declined to answer any of our questions, deftly deflecting them. He wouldn't even tell us how he had heard of our ministry.

His appearance suggested that he lived on the streets and the address he gave on his questionnaire was in a neighboring city. Surprisingly, at the deliverance session he was very well groomed, smartly dressed in a beautifully tailored suit, with a crisp, white shirt and tie. I courteously asked him to remove his suit coat, explaining to him that since we use anointing oil on our hands (and sometimes even pour it on a person's head), it is in the person's best interest. He refused, even getting a bit defiant.

As we have said, before we start a deliverance service, we always pray over the anointing oil and ask God to make it a symbol of the blood of Jesus. Believe me, it works! We never know what we will encounter during deliverance and the devils are scared to death of the blood of Jesus!

As I mentioned, this gentleman refused to remove his jacket for some reason and as we were praying for him, he bent over and I saw "the reason." He had a shoulder holster with a gun in it on his right side! I could hardly wait to tell Paul about the gun. He wasn't surprised, at all. Because he had seen a gun on the other side! Think of it! This man came into that deliverance service carrying two guns (which we assume were loaded) and we know that the Lord protected us from evil!

As we were praying for this man, the Lord revealed to me that the name "Gabriel Peace" that he had given to us was an assumed name. And in a startling development, as Paul was praying for him, he fell on his knees and begged Paul to forgive him. Forgive him for what? He didn't say, but he was obviously terrified and ran out of the room.

We do not know for certain why that man was sent to us, but we do know that he was up to no good! Even though we are sure he didn't get deliverance, we do know that the devils in him got stirred up. If the devils did leave while he was in the room (because of the anointing), they surely came back because they know they have a legal right to stay.

Whatever this man's intentions were, he didn't hurt us in any way. Why? Because we had a hedge of protection around us—through the blood of Jesus!

ANGEL ESCORT—CLAIRE

We held group training sessions for church leaders every three months and they came from all over the United States and many foreign countries. Bobbi attended with her husband, a pastor, from a midwestern state, and told us a remarkable story. As Paul was praying for a woman and commanding a demon to come out of her, the woman let out a bloodcurdling scream! At the same moment this woman screamed, Bobbi saw two angels come through a wall with tremendous speed, grab the demon, and take it with them out the same wall. She told us that this was the only time she had ever actually seen a demon or an angel.

Several months later, Bobbi and her husband invited us to come and minister in their church. This visit opened our eyes to some awesome truths and literally turned our whole ministry around. This couple has taught us so much and one of the basic truths pertained to breaking and keeping vows. The Lord had revealed to them the importance of confessing and asking forgiveness for breaking vows and covenants that you have made before Him. For example, the vows of marriage, joining a church, entering into contracts. Due to them and their anointed insights, we have broadened our horizons when it comes to warfare ministry.

HAUNTED HOUSE—CLAIRE

Debbie called us from another state and offered to pay all our expenses if we would come and pray for her. A friend from her church who had attended one of our deliverance conferences took all our manuals and tapes back to her.

At the time Debbie contacted us, she sent us an autobiography that outlined a tragic life. Fifteen years previous to her calling us, she had been left a quadriplegic due to injuries in an automobile accident. She had lost a dear sister, a brother, and a former husband in *separate* automobile accidents. Actually, because of the book, we felt almost like we knew her before we met her.

For many years, Debbie had been terrorized every night by strange occurrences in her home. As soon as the sun went down, doors started opening and closing, and she could hear voices and the sounds of large furniture being pushed around in the upper level of her house. Sometimes her little dog would literally fly across the room with great force. It got so bad that she could see people standing over her in her bedroom. Fear gripped her constantly!

We were met at the airport by Debbie's husband, David, an extremely handsome young man driving a white Jeep. David checked us into the hotel, took us to lunch, and talked to us about everything going on. He obviously loved his wife and spoke of her with great tenderness. He also told us about their beautiful, ten-year-old daughter who had the same sweet, kind personality of her mother.

You might wonder if we had any anxiety about what we might face in that house. After all, we knew we were going into a haunted house where people we had never met were being terrorized. The answer is simple: *we place our trust in God because He is the power that does the deliverance through us*!

David filled us in on details about the house. A beautiful, two-story mansion with a large attic and spacious cellar, it had been a convalescent home before they bought it.

As soon as we entered the house, we felt a strong presence of evil. We immediately anointed the house with oil and commanded evil spirits to leave! When we went to the attic, there was such a presence of evil that Paul's hair stood on end, he said. He began to pray in a strong way, but suddenly he got very loud and commanding, praying with more authority than I had ever seen! I could tell by looking at him that he really meant business. We also went to the cellar and anointed that area. Next we went to Debbie's bedroom to talk to her.

Because of Debbie's handicap, she had to lie totally flat on the bed. She was an extremely likable, lovely woman with a tremendous amount of charisma. We were able to see why she had so many, many friends who loved her and cared for her.

As we prayed for Debbie, a lot of things were revealed. As she had related in her book, her sister, brother, and former husband had died but what she did not understand was that the spirits that had lived in each of them had come into her upon their deaths. However, she actually had received the spirits of *four* persons. The fourth one was a familiar spirit that had come down through the inherited bloodline that had lived in her great-grandmother in the 1800's. Every time she would see a picture of that era, she would be overcome by an overwhelming urge to go back to that particular time. She would want to wear the clothes they wore then, fix her hair in those styles, and wear the jewelry. What a mess! How could you ever know the real YOU when so many multi-personalities were present?

Even though Debbie could not move her body, she would twist her head around during the deliverance. The spirits obviously were very angry at our coming to free her and at one point, a demon spoke to me through her, saying, "Get your hands off me!" A demon kept saying to Paul, "I HATE YOU! I HATE YOU!"

The Lord gave us discernment about some curses that had been put on her. When we broke the curses and told the demons to leave, they replied, "NO, there are too many of us." One demon said, "You don't know how long I've been here," and another said, "I will just hide." We heard another one say, "You don't know me." These demons were extremely abusive to us and we had a real fight on our hands. Regardless of how many demons there were or how long they had been there, they DID LEAVE and Debbie was delivered!

Immediately after her deliverance, Debbie remarked that she was experiencing feeling in her back that she had not felt since her accident. She was happy and joyous, and her countenance changed! She had received a glorious and victorious deliverance and the evil spirits that had haunted that house for years were miraculously removed!

We talked to Debbie the following week and she told us that she felt so free. What a change in her life! She had a tremendous hunger for the Word of God and she just wanted to get closer and closer to Jesus! In fact, she told us that she was no longer interested in soap operas on television—she just desired more of Jesus!

EERIE VOICE—CLAIRE

During another group seminar session, I was praying for a woman when suddenly I heard a strange, shrill sound permeate the room. It was a high-pitched sound, almost like a stringed instrument. I thought the tape in the recorder must be jammed and was "squealing." But when I checked the machine, everything was all right. Next, I looked around the room to see if I could get a clue and, to my surprise, I saw Paul and some other people gathered around Michael.

Michael was a muscular, striking-looking young man, with sandy hair and beautiful green eyes. I moved closer and saw that he was in a trance-like state and the shrill sound was coming from him. The strange thing was, he was speaking but his mouth was not moving at all. The voice seemed to be rising from deep inside his throat and we all knew that a demon was speaking through him. The sound was so eerie that it could not possibly be originating from a human. IT WAS A DEMONIC SPIRIT!

We have found that whenever a demon has completely taken over a person, you can usually bring the person back to himself by asking him a question. I got close enough for Michael to hear me and asked, "Michael, what is my name?" He turned his head very slowly, almost in a bobbing motion, and looking straight at me, he said, "Your name is Claire." Paul then asked him the same question. Again Michael moved his head slowly and deliberately, looked at Paul and said, "Your name is Paul."

Assuming that Michael had come back to himself, I went on to pray for someone else and Paul and others stayed to pray with Michael. Later they told me that the demon spoke after I walked away and said, "She was trying to trick Michael; she was using reverse psychology and it almost worked!" Every word that came out of his mouth was in a high-pitched, whining voice and was very demonic.

We have faithful helpers who pray with us, and two of those men stayed with Michael for several more hours until the demon left. It was not easy to deal with him. In fact, before the demon would leave, they had to get Michael to come back to himself and repeat the sinner's prayer. Then he got his deliverance! His countenance immediately changed so dramatically that everyone who saw him made comments about the alteration of his features.

We have a follow-up session the following day during these group sessions on HOW TO STAY FREE. Those who came back that day hardly recognized Michael. For the first three days of the seminar, he never spoke to anyone and looked bored (or even like he was sleeping) during the sessions. Now he bounced into the room with a beautiful smile on his face and was outgoing and friendly to everyone. You would have thought they were all his best friends! GOD CAN DO ANYTHING!

FREEWAY, HERE I COME!—CLAIRE

Beth was extremely sophisticated and fashionable but also very reserved. A true lady, she exuded confidence even though she was quite restrained. I ran into her in the hall of the church one morning and she spoke to me in very hushed tones, "Could I speak with you privately in your office?"

She shared with me that she had become so controlled by a spirit of fear that she couldn't even drive her car. She had her driver's license and knew perfectly well how to drive, but if she got behind the wheel of her car, panic seized her. She was becoming almost a recluse because she couldn't leave home unless someone drove her.

On the day we prayed for deliverance for Beth, the demon was furious! Through Beth's eyes, it glared at us with fierceness and wrath. There was fire in Beth's eyes and the demon obviously was defying us. But we prayed IN THE AUTHORITY OF THE NAME OF JESUS. Beth fixed her stare on us and I remember thinking, "I wonder if fire is going to come of her nose!" That demon put up a fierce battle, but Beth was gloriously set free!

We knew that the spirit of fear had left her and we wanted to prove it to her. We offered to give her a ride home because she had not driven over to the office, and when we all got out to our car, I threw her my car keys and said, "Get in! You're going to drive!" She hesitated until I told her that she needed to show the devil who was boss! That motivated her.

We had bought a new car and, I must admit, I had to conceal some doubts that kept creeping up. Paul gave me a slightly concerned look, then just seemed to resign himself to the inevitable—whatever it might be. As we got into the car, I spoke reassuring words to her and after she starting driving, I told her to take the freeway entrance. She quietly said she had never driven on the freeway and I said, very calmly,

"Don't worry; it's a piece of cake!" She was absolutely fantastic! At first she was pretty cool, then she got so excited. "I'm doing this! I'm doing this! I can't believe I am really doing this!"

The wonderful end to this story is that Beth has been driving ever since, over two years, and she just bought herself a new car. The devil had tried to hold her back from ministry by keeping her bound up by fear, but it didn't work. GOD HAD A BETTER PLAN!

For I know the thoughts that I think toward you, saith the Lord, thoughts of peace, and not of evil, to give you an expected end. (Jeremiah 29:11)

STRIP TEASE DURING CHURCH—CLAIRE

Let me share a simple truth: devils get very uncomfortable when they are around the anointing of the Holy Spirit and they will manifest. Many churches flowing in the anointing do not have a deliverance ministry but they will! How can I make such a blanket statement? Because there is a dramatic increase in demonic activity in the world today, and many people who attend church are in bondage. Therefore, deliverance ministry is becoming more urgently needed.

There are several factors that have contributed to this increased demonic activity. More and more people have been exposed to much of the occult through video games, television, psychics, palm readers, witchcraft, movies, and books. We in the church are going to have to know and understand spiritual warfare and deliverance in order to help others out of their bondage.

We recently encountered such an incident in our church. At the end of a strongly anointed service, people lined the altar. Some knelt, confessing their sins; others were on their faces before the Lord, praising and worshipping Him. I noticed a lady begin to "waltz" her way through the people up to the altar. She was dressed totally in white, white pants, white blouse, and she was barefoot. She danced on her tiptoes up the stairway that led to the platform and confronted our pastor, "I don't believe in your God!" Interestingly, her mouth did not move when she spoke. The pastor immediately called for us to come to the platform and we got her to go with us into an area on the side.

Paul began to bind up the spirits in her and things got crazy! Those devils looked out of her eyes with more hate than I think I have ever seen and it took two strong ushers to subdue her.

The orchestra was playing praise music with a strong rhythmic beat and this seemed to trigger something in her. She began to sway and move in a very sexual way and before anyone knew what was going on, she began taking off her white pants. She was not wearing underwear! Everyone sprang into action. Ushers dashed around trying to find something to hold in front of her to shield her from the congregation's eyes. Can you imagine going to church and seeing a strip tease show?

I hurriedly tried to maneuver her pants back up over her hips, but this was a real chore because of the battle she put up. She had fixed her eyes on my eyes in an evil stare, and I knew she was trying to do something evil. "Don't do that!" I commanded her, and I put my hand between her face and mine. She had acted wild before, but that made her totally crazy!

Finally I got her pants back on her and got her out of the area. She had left her shoes in the car, probably so that she could remove her pants more easily, so I encouraged her to go with me to the car to get her shoes. There was a man sitting in her very expensive, new car and I knew in my heart that he was the mastermind of this whole episode. She got in the car with him and they turned up the music and lit up cigarettes. Two ushers and I stayed by the car just in case she tried her "strip tease act" again in the parking lot while people were leaving the church. As we stood by the car, I knew they were trying to put curses on me, and the evil was very powerful! They finally left and everything got back to normal.

HERPES HEALED!—CLAIRE

Darlene, a well-groomed, middle-aged lady approached us at a seminar we were teaching at a Baptist church in Central Florida. She seemed pleasant but her face was sad, and marked with the lines of hard living.

Darlene insisted on seeing us privately for counseling, and we could see that she desperately needed deliverance. In talking with us later, she gave a history of a life of torment, abuse, guilt, and hopelessness. Her father had been "pastor" of a religious cult in a Northern state which practiced incest and other types of sexual misconduct. Total control was part of the cult, and members had to submit to all kinds of perverted activities. Darlene's childhood had been as horrible as anyone could ever imagine!

Darlene called on the morning of her scheduled deliverance session, crying so hard that we could hardly understand her. She had just come from her physician who had informed her that she had an extremely virulent case of herpes. Darlene was born again and had been married for over fifteen years. She had never had any evidence of herpes before and she was completely devastated at the news.

Darlene came to her session but she was armed! She carried a can of Lysol spray, a pair of gloves, some antibacterial soap and a sheet to put over her chair. *Her voice* kept telling us how dirty she was, but we knew a demon spirit was actually speaking through her.

The first thing we did in our prayer time with Darlene was break the power of the medications she had in her system, because she was taking all kinds of mind-altering drugs. (We have learned to do this, because medications can hinder the deliverance.) Also, as we have said, multi-personalities can hinder a deliverance, so we direct our attention to these at the onset of the session.

As he always does, Paul was holding Darlene's hands as he began to pray, but she pulled away from him, slipped out of her chair, and sat on the floor. She shut her eyes and pursed her lips so tightly that white showed around her lips.

Then Darlene began crawling! With her eyes still shut, she felt her way over to the wall, then followed the wall down to the corner, where she slumped into a fetal position. Frankly, we were unsure what to do at this point, as she would not respond to us no matter what we did or said. I felt impressed to pour anointing oil on the palm of my hand and press my palm to her mouth. When I did so, her eyes opened wide, her mouth flew open, and we were able to deal with the demon that had caused her to do all that.

Several other things happened in that deliverance session, as well. Darlene had many demonic personalities and as we prayed, all but one left. We were not able to get discernment on what that one was and we knew better than to proceed without making sure that it was gone. After waiting on the Lord, He revealed to us that we were dealing with a "shut down" personality. When Darlene was being sexually abused as a child, she would "shut down" her own personality and pretend to be somewhere else. The pain of what was happening to her was so extreme that she "became" someone else. That had allowed a multi-personality to enter.

Darlene could not trust anyone when she was a little girl; her only friend was the girl in the mirror. She would line up all her little toys, then she and "Janie," the girl in the mirror, would play. We had to break an ungodly soul tie she had developed with "Janie" and then we had to get rid of the multi-personality named Janie.

Darlene also had many phobic fears. When we called out a spirit of "fear of relationships," the spirit spoke through her and asked, "Who told you I was here?" When we called out a spirit of guilt, it spoke through her and said, "She kicked me out—and now I'm back." When we called out a spirit of shame, the spirit spoke and said, "She's shameful— she's shameful!"

A spirit of nightmares was extremely violent with Darlene. It cut off her windpipe, trying to kill her, and she desperately clutched her throat. I grabbed the anointing oil again, poured it into the palm of my hand, and put my hand on her throat. Immediately she began to breathe!

When we commanded the spirit of herpes to leave her, the demon in her went wild, saying, "She's nasty! She's nasty!" But the demon *had* to leave in the Name of Jesus!

Darlene experienced a glorious deliverance and we didn't see her again for several months. However, a couple of weeks after her deliverance, we had lunch with her pastor and his wife. They gave us a glowing report of Darlene's health. The morning after the deliverance session, her herpes had disappeared without a trace.

An interesting sideline is that we didn't know that herpes was a demon spirit. It has always been our practice to call out the spirits of infirmity by the names of the disease a person has. We figure that if the disease is caused by a demonic influence, it will leave; if not, then it will stay. What do you have to lose for trying!

STRANGE MANIFESTATIONS

Janet's dimpled smile was charming and she was extremely winsome. She dressed conservatively but fashionably and spoke to us in a very intelligent manner. She had asked to see us because she had been hypnotized twenty years earlier by a person in the occult, and that demon still had control over her mind.

During deliverance, Paul called out spirits of occult to leave her and her eyes began to roll around in opposite directions. One eye would go to the left and the other to the right, AT THE SAME TIME! This is physically impossible to do—but it was happening! Janet was set free, but during that session we witnessed another strange manifestation from demonic forces.

We are constantly amazed at all the different manifestations of the satanic kingdom that we see. People also tell us stories about things that have happened to them when they have burned "their list." Let me explain. When we counsel people, we ask them to make a list of all occult activities they have ever been involved in. We instruct them to renounce all the things on their list with a proclamation that we provide them. After they have done this, they are to burn the list just to show the physical world what is happening in the spiritual realm. And this is where we get some fascinating stories.

Some people have told us that their list exploded like a firecracker when they put a match to it. Some have said that it has taken two books of matches to start the fire and then burn it. Others have had the list turn a strange color when it became ashes, while some lists have emitted a terrible odor. Unbelievable as it may seem, some individuals have even heard screams as their paper burned. The list of manifestations goes on and on.

I recently received a "chain letter" in the mail with a warning that if I did not send the letter on to thirty people, I would have very bad luck. The letter cited examples of people who didn't forward the letter who had died or lost a loved one or suffered financial disaster. Conversely, the letter said that if I forwarded it within 72 hours, *much good luck* would come my way. Anyone with even the slighted spiritual discernment could see that this is extremely demonic in nature. You see, if you forward the letter, you open yourself up to spirits of occult and fear. And if you believe what the crazy letter tells you about misfortune befalling you if you *do not* send it on, then you can open yourself up to a curse *because of the spirit of fear* coming on you which makes you fear that a curse *will befall you*. We know that curses can't hurt you, but *fear of a curse can be deadly!*

The Lord revealed to us who had sent the letter. Paul and I applied some anointing oil to the paper, took it to the kitchen sink, and burned it!

Stay far away from anything to do with the occult because you could actually be calling on demons. If you are already involved in occult and New Age activities, you won't have to worry. God is big enough to clean up any mess and set you free!

DEMON LEFT QUIETLY

In the preceding pages, we have related cases where we have seen manifestations when the demons left. It is important to note that some of our *most profound* cases of deliverance have had no manifestations whatsoever. This has nothing to do with us; it all depends upon whether or not the devil wants to show off on the way out or not. Many times they will leave with a streak of pain, but that does not last long. We do not try to stop the demons from manifesting (unless they try to hurt the person or us). The reason is simple:

Sometimes the person being delivered needs the assurance of experiencing a demonic manifestation in order to know that they have received deliverance. They need to be sure the demons are gone!

People who don't feel anything because the demons leave quietly sometimes have more difficulty realizing that they have actually received deliverance. It may takes weeks for them to realize that the things that had them bound are no longer there. We get fascinating testimonies from these individuals, even though their deliverance was not dramatic. One of the most common reactions is that the person can't believe the way they now react to certain situations compared to how they behaved earlier. **Then they finally realize the total freedom and victory that God brought into their lives.**

OUR GREAT COMMISSION

We are determined to fulfill the Great Commission God has given to us. We believe in evangelism! As we minister to people, our first mission is to lead them to Jesus Christ. The Bible tells us that we must get rid of the weight and sin. Through evangelism, the sin is gone and we are washed by the blood of Jesus.

Wherefore seeing we also are compassed about with so great a cloud of witnesses, let us lay aside every weight, and the sin which doth so easily beset us, and let us run with patience the race that is set before us. (Heb. 12:1)

Even though you get born again and washed by the blood of Jesus, you can still be burdened down with fear, grief, depression, rejection, addiction, lust, and many other "weights." If these weights are not removed, a Christian can be under so much heaviness that they become discouraged and finally say, "It's no use!" However, through a prayer of deliverance, these weights can be removed and you can walk in beautiful freedom. You will begin to soar in your relationship with God. In many deliverance sessions, we have seen healings take place when the spirits of infirmity leave.

I am he that liveth, and was dead; and, behold, I am alive for evermore, Amen; and have the keys of hell and of death. (Rev. 1:18)

And I will give unto thee the keys of the kingdom of heaven: and whatsoever thou shalt bind on earth shall be bound in heaven: and whatsoever thou shalt loose on earth shall be loosed in heaven. (Matt. 16:19)

And Jesus came and spake unto them, saying, All power is given unto me in heaven and in earth. (Matt. 28:18)

Every born-again Christian should be eager to fulfill the Great Commission, as Jesus did. We, the Body of Christ, have the power and authority, through Jesus Christ, to bind and loose every devil in satan's kingdom. This weapon, this authority, is implemented by our tongue. We simply have to command the spirit to be loosed and it is done! The scriptures tell us how Christ commanded demons to be bound and leave an individual's body. Jesus spoke with *authority* because He knew He had the authority!

Today the Body of Christ has that same AUTHORITY through the Name of Jesus Christ. Jesus told us, *Verily, verily, I say unto you, He that believeth on me, the works that I do shall he do also; and greater works than these shall he do; because I go unto my father. (John 14:12)*

The average Christian does not use this God-given authority and some are afraid to fight the good fight. The Bible instructs us to be aggressive in this spiritual battle: *And from the days of John the Baptist until now the kingdom of heaven suffereth violence, and the violent take it by force. (Matt. 11:12)*

If we, as born-again Christians, are to become the violent who take this world by force, we cannot run from the fight! If we run, we will get beaten up, stepped on, and run over by evil spirits. It is time that we become MIGHTY WARRIORS in God's Kingdom and begin to fulfill ALL of the Great Commission.

It seems that today there is more demonic activity on planet Earth than at any other time since the beginning of mankind. Our battles are against spiritual *entities. For we wrestle not against flesh and blood, but against principalities, against powers, against the rulers of the darkness of this world, against spiritual wickedness in high places. (Eph. 6:12)*

If your child is rebellious, realize that a spirit in involved; then bind up the spirit of rebellion in your child!

114

When your coworkers talk about you, causing a poor work environment, bind up that spirit of gossip and backbiting. You have the authority, so exercise it!

If you have a spouse who is unfaithful, bind up the spirit of lust and seduction. Again, God wants you to use the authority that He has given you!

We also have the authority to bind ruling spirits over our homes, families, churches, cities, businesses and this nation. Be militant and aggressive in God's Kingdom!

This is all part of the Great Commission. We need to be like Paul the Apostle. *I have fought a good fight, I have finished my course, I have kept the faith. (II Tim. 4:7)*

We are in a spiritual battle! Don't be caught unprepared without proper knowledge. You need to know who the enemy is and how he operates. What are you going to do with the knowledge that God has given you? Be strong, be bold, and face the devil head-on!

If you do not know Christ as your personal Savior, the following verses will show you how to receive Jesus into your heart and be born again.

For God so loved the world, that he gave his only begotten Son, that whosoever believeth in him should not perish, but have everlasting life. (John 3:16)

That if thou shalt confess with thy mouth the Lord Jesus, and shalt believe in thine heart that God hath raised him from the dead, thou shalt be saved. For with the heart man believeth unto righteousness; and with the mouth confession is made unto salvation. (Romans 10:9, 10)

If you want to make a decision to believe in Jesus Christ and ask Him to be your Savior, PRAY THIS PRAYER:

> *Heavenly Father, I ask you to forgive me for my sins and anything I have ever done to offend you.*
>
> *I believe that Jesus is your only begotten Son, and that He died for my sins.*
>
> *Please come into my heart and be lord of my life.*
>
> *In Jesus' Name. Amen.*

We believe that we will soon experience the greatest reunion in the history of mankind! The saints will meet the Lord in the air!

His lord said unto him, Well done, thou good and faithful servant: thou hast been faithful over a few things, I will make thee ruler over many things: enter thou into the joy of thy lord. (Matt. 25:21)

And he said unto them, I beheld Satan as lightning fall from heaven.

Behold, I give unto you power to tread on serpents and scorpions, and over all the power of the enemy: and nothing shall by any means hurt you.

Notwithstanding in this rejoice not, that the spirits are subject unto you; but rather rejoice, because ***your names are written in heaven.***

Luke 10:18-20

Paul and Claire Hollis minister nationally and have seen thousands of people freed from demonic influence. They each hold a degree of Ph.D. in Clinical Christian Psychology, and conduct private and group counseling sessions. They also conduct seminars and teach a School of Deliverance.

Other books by Paul and Claire

THIS MEANS WAR is a complete guide to the teachings of Christ on deliverance. This book will take you through a step-by-step process to eliminate any demonic strongholds within your own life. Sadly, deliverance has been treated almost like a forbidden topic in the church realm. *THIS MEANS WAR* teaches in great depth everything you always wanted to know about demon warfare and the supernatural, but have been afraid to ask!

THE LIGHT Go on an adventure with JJ and Lynn as they visit a mysterious town. The curtain gets pulled back on some fascinating, supernatural things that have been covered over for years. JJ and Lynn get into trouble and find themselves in life-threatening situations. Get to know Lana, who states, "I hate those two! Our leader hates them, too. And his number-one goal is to completely destroy them!"

DELAYED INVASION A U.S. military crew in Germany mysteriously intercepts a plot by demon entities to overthrow the governments of the world by disguising themselves as beings from outer space. Go with JJ and Lynn as they visit Washington, DC and get caught up in the middle of the invasion plans.

DECEIVED Worldwide revival is taking place on planet Earth and people everywhere are uniting, with Christ as the common denominator. Satan and Lana have devised a plan that cannot fail! Satan tells Lana, "I want you to pick out two men, one in the political arena and the other in religion. Set them up as world leaders then, when the time is right, I will enter one of them just like I did Judas Iscariot. Then I WILL RULE THE WORLD!" Even as unseen entities take over the world, the majority of people are unaware of what is going on.

If these books are not yet available in your local bookstore, order them direct by e-mail, calling, or faxing our Tampa office.

Warfare Plus Ministries offers many tape series on special demonic warfare issues and mini-books on individual stronghold forces. For a listing of our ministry tapes, manuals and other material, visit our web site or write to us. You may also request a product order form at the same address.

If you are interested in attending a group seminar or want to schedule a group seminar in your local church, please call or write to us:

Paul and Claire Hollis
Warfare Plus Ministries, Inc.
PMB #206
4577 Gunn Highway
Tampa, FL 33624 USA
(813) 265-2379
Fax : (813) 908-0228
E-mail: WarfareP@aol.com
Web Site: www.warfareplus.com

Product Order Form

Product Number	Description	Quantity	Unit Price	Total Cost
BOOKS				
WP-101	This Means War		$12.95	
WP-102	Demon Slayers		$11.95	
WP-103	The Light		$11.95	
WP-104	Delayed Invasion		$11.95	
WP-105	Deceived		$12.95	
AUDIOS				
WP-201	Expose & Expel Demon Power (4 Tapes)		$20.00	
WP-202	Inner Healing/Spiritual D. (4 Tapes)		$20.00	
WP-203	Don't Get Caught In Satan's Web		$10.00	
WP-204	Are You Cursed? (2 Tapes)		$10.00	
WP-205	Power & Authority Over Evil (2 Tapes)		$10.00	
WP-206	If I'm Supposed To Be Gay …(2 Tapes)		$10.00	
VIDEOS				
WP-301	Expose & Expel (4 Videos)		$80.00	
WP-302	Inner Healing/Spiritual D. (4 Videos)		$80.00	
WP-303	Deliverance From Satan's Torment		$20.00	
WORKBOOKS				
WP-401	Expose & Expel Demon Power		$20.00	
WP-402	Inner Healing/Spiritual Deliverance		$20.00	
WP-403	New Beginnings In Jesus Christ		$20.00	

SUB TOTAL

Method Of Payment:
- ☐ Visa
- ☐ MasterCard
- ☐ Check

Credit Card Number:
_____

Expiration Date:
_____

Shipping & Handling
$10.00 & Less	$3.00
$10.01-25.00	$4.00
$25.02-40.00	$5.00
$40.01-60.00	$6.00
$60.01-75.00	$7.00
$75.01 or more	$9.00
USA RATES

Shipping & handling (see chart)

TOTAL

Please Print Clearly

Name _____
Address _____
City _____
State _____
Zip _____

Send To:
Warfare Plus Ministries
4577 Gunn Highway, PMB 206
Tampa, FL 33624

Fax: (813) 908-0228
E-Mail: WarfareP@aol.com